SECRET PLACES OF WESTERN NEW YORK

25 SCENIC HIKES

Written by
BRUCE KERSHNER, JENNIFER HILLMAN
and **WILLIAM MCKEEVER**

Photographs and Illustrations by
BRUCE KERSHNER and **COURTNEY GRIM**

Reedy Press
PO Box 5131
St. Louis, MO 63139
www.reedypress.com

Library of Congress Control Number: 2021952872
ISBN: 9781681063683

Cover design: Eric Marquard
Interior design: Eric Marquard and Linda Eckels

Printed in the United States of America
24 25 26 5 4 3

Dedication

This book is dedicated to Helene Kershner.
Thank you for believing, then and now.

Swallow Hallow Path

SECRET PLACES OF WESTERN NEW YORK

25 SCENIC HIKES

REEDY PRESS

Contents

Stella Niagara
5-mile meadow

Acknowledgments

A book like this takes decades to create and draws from the experiences and expertise of many communities, partnerships, and individuals.

The support from our nature, environmental, tourism, and advocacy agencies in providing access, performing fact-checking, and leading us on guided hikes was overwhelming. In particular, we would like to thank Jajean Rose-Burney of the Western New York Land Conservancy; Mike Radomski from Outside Chronicles and #HikeWNY; Karen Fashana at Visit Buffalo Niagara; Libby Woock at Destination Niagara; Elizabeth Licata, editor of *Buffalo Spree* magazine and author of S*ECRET Buffalo; Ga'Vintay McGhee,* photography work-study student at Medaille College; Helene, Libby, and Joshua Kershner; and Sallie Randolph.

A special thank you to Courtney Grim, our dear friend, 25-plus-year hiking partner, and photographer extraordinaire! Your photos show the world how beautiful Western New York is.

It's been 28 years since Bruce Kershner published *Secret Places: Scenic Treasures of Western New York and Southern Ontario*. Yet, not only is the book not forgotten, it's revered. We acknowledge his tireless effort to share, protect, and advocate for these and all "secret places" everywhere.

—Jennifer Hillman and Bill McKeever

We thank Mother Nature and her Creator for giving us these treasures of nature at our doorstep and for making our world full of wonder, fascination, and reverence.

—Bruce Kershner

Foreword

My father always took me on his weekend hikes. For him, they were often research trips, but, for me, they were special adventures. My childhood memories are of hiking through the woods holding his hand and watching him wander off the trail to check out an interesting plant or to measure the girth of a tree. He told me to listen carefully for the amazing creatures that come out at night and to "put my eyes in my feet" and step over tree roots in the dark.

His passion for finding unusual places and enthusiasm for the natural world led him to share these discoveries with others. He led hikes to Reinstein Woods and gave lectures about the incredible ancient forests that he discovered. People told him, "You should publish a book!" Eventually, he did. *Secret Places of Western New York and Southern Ontario* was a wild success.

As one of the nation's leading experts on old-growth forests, he worked tirelessly to identify and save pockets of old-growth trees throughout the Northeast. When my father became ill and surrendered to the reality that death was his next great adventure, he told us that he only feared for two things: his family and his trees.

He need not have feared.

His name now lives on through four grandchildren. I now hold their hands as they join me on special adventures to "secret places."

Through my father's work, old-growth trees were saved at Zoar Valley, Reinstein Woods, DeVeaux Woods, College Lodge, and too many more places to mention.

The spirit of my father is basking in the sunlight, high up in an old-growth tree, excited to see a new generation of hikers discover his secret places. As my father autographed his books:

May the Forest Be with You!

Libby

– Libby Kershner

Reinstein Woods
old-growth trees

Introduction

In 1994, Bruce Kershner published *Secret Places: Scenic Treasures of Western New York and Southern Ontario* and sparked the region's love affair with our outdoor treasures. He encouraged generations of local residents and visitors to Western New York to get up, get out, and explore nature.

More than that, he helped instill a love and appreciation for giant old trees, unusual plants, and the environment that sheltered and sometimes hid them.

His enthusiasm was boundless and contagious. Through books and advocacy, he inspired others, and, today, many of these secret and not-so-secret places are better known with new or strengthened protections, allowing them to continue to be discovered and appreciated.

Jennifer Hillman and Bill McKeever benefited from knowing Bruce, and, like many fellow nature lovers, they were inspired to "hike the book" when they first started dating. Bill worked closely with Bruce for several years at the Buffalo Audubon Society—Bill as its executive director and Bruce as a board member and chair of the Society's Conservation Committee. Jennifer, Bill, and Secret Places photographer Courtney Grim have funny and fond memories of Bruce-led interpretive hikes at the annual Allegany Nature Pilgrimages.

Jennifer and Bill's lifelong passion for connecting with nature rekindled when, years later, married and with young children, they dusted off their old and tattered copy of *Secret Places* and began sharing these out-of-the way places with their kids.

After years of gifting copies of *Secret Places* to friends, coworkers, and new arrivals to Western New York, *Secret Places* could no longer be found! To continue sharing these treasures with others, Jennifer and Bill partnered with the Kershner estate to launch this new book in the *Secret Places* series with updates to the original locations and several new secret places to explore.

We hope this book inspires you to "go take a hike."

Happy trails!

CANADA
Niagara Falls, NY
③ Artpark
Buffalo
LAKE ERIE
Sister Beach
I-90
Canadaway Creek
25
RT 60
17
18
20
21 College Lodge
I-90
I-86
Jamestown
RT 62
I-86
24
I-190

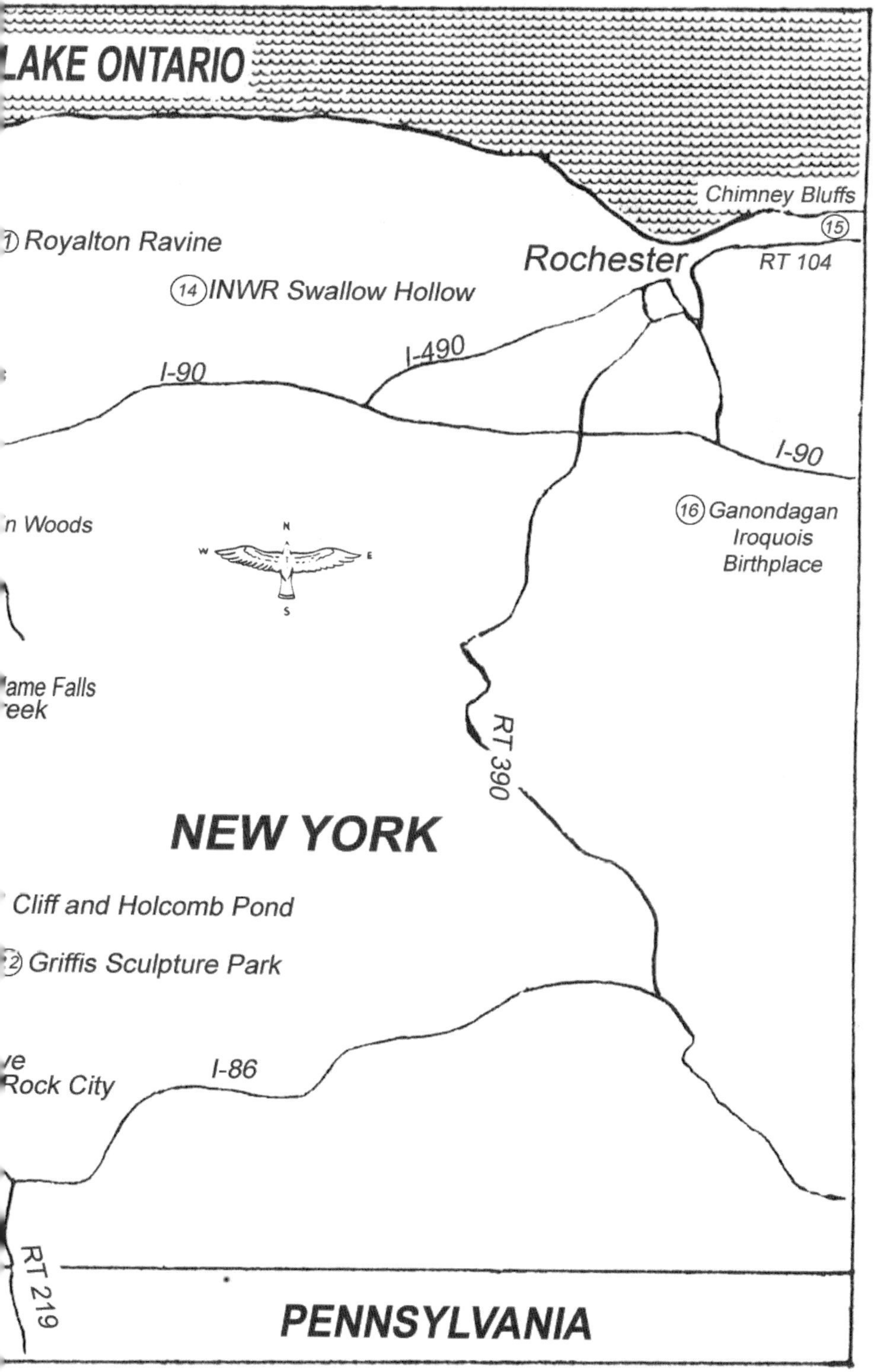

Maps are for overview only; not for directional purposes and not to scale.

How to Use This Book

The hikes in this book are listed by region and encompass the counties that make up Western New York (WNY) and slightly beyond. Every hike in the book can be reached within a two-hour drive in WNY.
The overview map will show you clusters of hikes, so you can plan on doing a few together or over a couple days.
The description of each hike provides GPS coordinates to the trailhead, along with the street and city to use in your mapping program. After all, you don't want to get lost before you get there. Always download the trail map from the land management entity or use a hiking app.

Plan your adventure based on the level of difficulty and trail distance. The level of difficulty is a simple scale of easy, moderate, and difficult. Choose hikes that match your experience and the experience of those accompanying you (including pets!).

The usage icons show what you can expect, such as fees, bathrooms, swimming allowed, dogs allowed, hunting allowed, and wheeled accessibility. The features section provides a quick overview of the outdoor experience.

Each hike will include a description of a few unique features, which are what make each hike a "Secret Place." In "The Hike" section, we guide you through the trail and point out where to find these unique features. Sometimes, we include a brief history of the location if it will enrich your outing.

At the end of each hike, we discuss seasonality considerations and make special gear suggestions to enhance your experience.

HIKING SAFETY, PREPARATION, AND SUGGESTED GEAR. The hikes in this guide feature different kinds of terrain for people and pets of different abilities. Paved trails can become wet and slippery. Creek beds can become mucky and rained out, and trails can become buggy and thorn-covered. These hazards are predictable, and you should plan for them.

WEAR APPROPRIATE FOOTWEAR. Don't be that person hiking in flimsy flip-flops! There is nothing worse than having your hike ruined by a blister or bashed toe. Wear hiking boots or shoes with ankle support that cover your entire foot. Wear wick-away socks to keep your feet dry. If you're planning for a creek hike or swim, pack water shoes, but wear hiking shoes.

COTTON KILLS. Cotton is great when you get off the trail. It's soft and feels lovely next to your skin. But on the trail, it holds in moisture from sweat, rain, and snow. When hiking, layer your clothes and keep polyester (not nylon) next to your skin. Wearing lightweight hiking pants in the summer will protect you from thorns and brambles that line the trails.

LEAVE WORD. Tell someone you're going hiking, where you're going, and when you expect to be back. Always sign into trailhead logs. Not only is this a safety precaution, but it also helps with funding allocations to our park systems and nonprofit preserves.

PACK A HIKING BAG. Always carry the following 10 essentials with you, according to the National Park Service (NPS.org):

Navigation: map, compass, and GPS system
Sun Protection: sunglasses, sunscreen, and hat
Insulation: jacket, hat, gloves, rain shell, and thermal underwear
Illumination: flashlight, lanterns, and headlamp
First-Aid Kit: buy a pre-made kit and modify/replace as needed
Fire: matches, lighter, and fire starters
Tools: knife, duct tape, rope
Nutrition: high-energy food that's easy to digest
Hydration: water and water treatment supplies
Emergency Shelter: even on a day hike, pack a space blanket
Extras: Bug protection (with DEET), walking stick

THE LEAVE NO TRACE SEVEN PRINCIPLES

Please protect the natural beauty and ecological integration of these secret places by practicing the Leave No Trace seven principles:

1. Plan Ahead and Prepare
2. Travel and Camp on Durable Surfaces
3. Dispose of Waste Properly
4. Leave What You Find
5. Minimize Campfire Impacts
6. Respect Wildlife
7. Be Considerate of Other Visitors

DISCLAIMER

The authors, contributors, and publishers of this guide assume no responsibility for errors or inaccuracies to this guide; for changes in weather, trail routes, or conditions; or for injuries, damages, or death resulting from the use of this guide, the trails, or the recreational facilities thereon.

HIKE AT YOUR OWN RISK!

Hike only after you have adequately planned and prepared for your trip. The use of this guide does not guarantee a safe and successful trip.

USAGE ICONS

- BATHROOM
- BIKING
- BIRDING
- CAMPING
- CAVE
- CREEK
- DISCOVER NIAGARA SHUTTLE
- EV CHARGING STATION
- FAMILIES
- FEES
- FISHING
- HIKING
- HISTORY BUFFS
- HUNTING
- LEASHED DOGS
- NATURE CENTER
- OLD-GROWTH TREES
- OUTDOOR ART
- PADDLING
- PLAYGROUND
- ROCKS/ GEOLOGICAL INTEREST
- SCENIC OVERLOOKS
- SCENIC VIEWS
- SNOWSHOEING
- SWIMMING/ SPLASHING
- WATERFALLS
- WHEELED VISITOR FRIENDLY
- XC SKIING (CROSS COUNTRY)

BEST SEASONS

- FALL
- WINTER
- SPRING
- SUMMER

Royalton Ravine Waterfall

1

Royalton Ravine and the 138-foot Swinging Bridge

LOCATION: Royalton Ravine Park, Gasport, NY
GPS: 43.186376, –78.577182

FEATURES: This scenic, wooded ravine along the edge of the Niagara Escarpment has a 138-foot wooden, swinging footbridge. As you cross over the stream below, the sway of the footbridge, along with the wave motion, is a hilarious sensation for kids and young-at heart explorers.

DISTANCE: 2 miles/out-and-back
LEVEL OF DIFFICULTY: Moderate
USAGE ICONS:

BEST SEASONS:

TRAIL MAP: At trailhead kiosk
MANAGED BY: Niagara County Parks Department

Royalton Ravine 138-foot Swinging Bridge

Feel the suspension bridge swing and undulate rhythmically back and forth like you're on a boat.

UNIQUE FEATURES

A 138-foot long swinging bridge: As the longest swinging bridge in the area, this bridge alone is enough reason to visit this park and is an experience not to be missed.

Belva Lockwood and Uriah McNall Homestead: Walk into the ruins of a pre–Civil War era homestead. Belva Lockwood is a notable part of American history. A former teacher and school principal locally, she became the first woman ever admitted to practice law before the Supreme Court and was the first woman to ever run for president of the United States (in both 1884 and 1888), significantly advancing the women's suffrage movement.

Royalton Falls: A scenic 25-foot drop waterfall that powered a 19th-century gristmill.

Stone Well Ruins: Find old ruins that were either from a well or cistern that provided water to the old homestead.

THE HIKE

After you park your vehicle, walk west across the lawn past the picnic shelters and toward the woods. This unmarked trail starts on top of a long berm with the pond on your left. As you approach the woods, an information kiosk will indicate the starting point of the trail system.

Follow the well-marked, red-blazed trail that leads to the left through the mature forest. As it quickly starts to descend into the woods, you'll see the yellow-roped lumber steps set into the trail that will bring you to the edge of the ravine. Continue to hike west (left), following the red trail markers. You'll pass over a 30-foot section of knobby tree roots above the grade of the trail, which led us to dub this section the "Royalton Ravine Roots" trail.

The trail goes through a maple and beech forest as it heads toward the cable bridge. Spanning 138 feet over the ravine is the **Swinging Foot Bridge** that is just three feet above the east branch of Eighteen Mile Creek.

As you cross the suspension bridge, it swings and undulates rhythmically back and forth. Kids and kids at heart love bouncing on it and making it rock. Try lying down in the center of the bridge while others bounce on the bridge, and you'll get wave motions like you're lying on a boat.

After crossing the bridge, continue up the ravine on the red trail, and you'll pass the carved heart on a maple tree. Stop for a moment to ponder the somewhat dubious connection between expressive love and tree destruction, and then continue uphill toward the waterfall and homestead sites.

Royalton Ravine Roots trail

Belva Lockwood and Uriah McNall homestead ruins

About a half-mile uphill, you'll come to the ruins of the pre–Civil War homestead of Belva Lockwood and Uriah McNall. Walk inside the homestead ruins to see where the front door, fireplace, and other structures were located. Although vandals have taken a toll over the years, the house is still intact enough that you can imagine what it looked like in the mid-1800s. Belva and Uriah operated a sawmill at the site and generated power from the nearby waterfall.

Just past the homestead on the left is Royalton Falls, with stone structures that likely served as impoundments of the water behind them to harness the energy for the sawmill. Look for the stone abutments on both sides at the top of the falls, which are the remains of a short bridge that crossed over the falls. The waterfall is delightful to behold in the spring as it cascades 25 feet over the Niagara Escarpment.

Take the yellow trail that starts on the side of the homestead near the "doorway." A short distance later, as the land dips from water runoff, look to your right to see the ruins of a circular stone well or cistern on the side of the hill.

The woods here are particularly pretty and filled with pines, mature birches, beeches, maples, and oaks. Continue to follow the yellow trail to the edge of the park property, and then turn right at the field; shortly after, the yellow trail ends at a neighboring apple orchard.

Double back on the yellow trail to return to the homestead, and then take a left back onto the red trail to come back to the trailhead.

PLANNING YOUR VISIT

Summer is a fun time to bring kids to hike in the creek from the swinging bridge up to the base of the waterfall. Unfortunately, the only way back is the way you came. On a hot summer day, a shaded creek walk is a good time for anyone. In the **fall**, the woods are ablaze with color and the yellow trail is stunning, with a mix of green pines, birches, oaks, and maples. The creek is just a trickle this time of year and mud should be minimal.

Winter and spring hiking will require ice spikes and boots. **Spring** is the best time of year to see the waterfall in its full glory; however, the trails may be difficult to navigate. If you just want to take a quick peek at the waterfall, park at the Kayner Road gated entrance and hike in about 0.25 mile.

HIKING DATES

HIKING NOTES

Stella Niagara 200-year-old
red oak witness tree

2

Five-mile Meadow and the Last Landing at Stella Niagara

LOCATION: Stella Niagara Preserve, Lower River Road, Lewiston, NY

GPS: 43.201848, –79.042373

FEATURES: This is the very spot where the British landed in 1813 to capture Fort Niagara. Its canoe landing site was a strategic setting for the native peoples who used the Niagara River for transport, trade, and fishing. Today, you can hike the natural meadow and view migrating birds, and see the tiniest church in Western New York.

DISTANCE: 1.4 miles/loop

LEVEL OF DIFFICULTY: Easy

USAGE ICONS:

BEST SEASONS:

TRAIL MAP: https://bit.ly/SPWNY1

MANAGED BY: Western New York Land Conservancy

See the phenomenal display of thousands of fireflies flash-dancing in the air.

UNIQUE FEATURES

Five-mile meadow: This local name is derived from the low, flat meadow five miles above Fort Niagara to the north. The five-mile meadow makes up 13 of the site's 29 acres and is 60 feet lower than the surrounding area, which made this the ideal spot for the British, French, and Native American peoples to use for water landings.

The native fauna has been restored to include natural grasses and nearly 100 native plant species that attract an abundant variety of Eastern bluebirds, warblers, turkey vultures, finches, Baltimore orioles, and a flock of **black vultures**—rare visitors from the south.

The Last Landing: This landing was known as Yeh-heh-weh-kwah-taw: "the place where they take the boats out." Heading upriver, it was the last best place to come ashore prior to reaching the impassable Niagara Falls.

Witness Tree: There are two mighty, old-growth oaks that are believed to be more than 200 years old and would have "witnessed" a British

Stella Niagara Miracle Chapel

Grotto of Bernadette of Lourdes

war party landing in 1813. While the 245-year-old white oak is pretty deep into the woods, the 200-year-old red oak is easily viewed as you walk from the Last Landing to the "Miracle Chapel on the River."

Spiritual sites: As you wander down the main path, the **Grotto of Bernadette of Lourdes** will reveal itself to the left of the service road. Still visited today by the Sisters of St. Francis, this is a spiritual site for quiet and meditative reflection. Take a moment to appreciate the artwork style in the grotto, which is also used inside the tiny **Miracle Chapel on the River**, and the **Kennedy Peace Memorial**, all notably decorated in sgraffito by Polish artist Joseph Slawinski, who brought this fresco like style of art to Western New York.

THE HIKE

The hike is 1.4 miles of a winding, loop trail that descends 80 feet from the Lower River Road to the Last Landing. Parking is across the street at the Senior Center lot at the northeastern corner of Pletcher Road and Lower River Road. The trails are prepared for universal access with wide paths and a gradual decline, but there is no suitable surface for wheeled access, and benches have not been placed for sitting and resting.

Follow the path as it slowly winds and descends through the meadow, past the **grotto**, the wetland, and the **Last Landing**. Before you reach the **Miracle Chapel on the River**, stop and appreciate the 200-year-old red oak **witness tree**.

The **Miracle Chapel on the River** is thought to be the tiniest religious structure in Western New York. The chapel claims two miracles. The first was in March 1955, when two winter storms converged from Lake Ontario to the north and Lake Erie from the south and created ice jams along the lower Niagara River. Miles of property along the lower river were destroyed, and although the icy flooding encased Five-mile Meadow, it never crossed the chapel's doorstep and it remained protected. This "miracle" made national news.

The second miracle happened when artist Joseph Slawinski was healed while creating the sgraffito on the chapel's ceiling. The artwork depicts St. Mary protecting the chapel during the ice jam of 1955. Although Slawinski was very ill when he started this commission, when the commission was done, he was healed.

The secured chapel's tiny interior and sgraffito ceiling can be seen through an arranged private WNY Land Conservancy tour.

As you circle around the trail and head back up toward the road, you'll find the final spiritual site on your right, the **Kennedy Peace Memorial**, built shortly after President John F. Kennedy was assassinated.

This leisurely stroll takes about an hour. If you have more time, pack a picnic lunch, sit for a bit along the river, and watch as all sorts of bird, aquatic, and human activity peacefully drift by while remembering the long-ago day when British soldiers stole ashore to wreak havoc.

PLANNING YOUR VISIT

This is a beautiful location for a **summer's** day or evening's stroll through the flowering meadow filled with fluttering, winged creatures everywhere (in other words, bring bug spray!). For a special **summer** treat, go on a June or July evening to see the phenomenal display of thousands of fireflies. **Fall** and **spring** welcome thousands of migratory birds passing through on their way south from Canada. In addition to the amazing array of ducks, 18 different gull species overwinter along the Niagara River.

Stella Niagara Landing

HIKING DATES

HIKING NOTES

Lewiston Queenston
Bridge at Artpark
State Park

3

Artpark: The Birthplace of Niagara

LOCATION: 499 S 4th Street, Lewiston, NY
GPS: 43.164878, –79.044473

FEATURES: Two hiking trails follow sections of the 7-mile portage trail early European settlers and native peoples traveled. This was to bypass the unpassable Niagara rapids and falls.

DISTANCE: 2.5 miles/loop
LEVEL OF DIFFICULTY: Easy to moderate
USAGE ICONS:

BEST SEASONS:

FEES: The grounds are free and open year-round, except during major events.

TRAIL MAP: https://bit.ly/SPWNY2
Niagara Gorge Trail map: https://bit.ly/SPWNY_NFGORGE
MANAGED BY: New York State Parks, Recreation and Historic Preservation

Artpark Niagara Gorge trail

Art is everywhere! Hike on the Sonic Trails, and then bang drums in a Percussion Garden.

UNIQUE FEATURES

Niagara Escarpment: This is the ancient birthplace of Niagara Falls. Over the past 12,000 years, **the Falls** have continued to migrate south as the Niagara River slowly erodes the rocks and sediment from the Niagara Escarpment.

Art in the Park: From the colorful striped parking lot, called Niagara 1979, to Sonic Trails and Percussion Gardens, Artpark is filled with full sensory experiences.

Lewiston-Queenston Bridge: You can't hike on this bridge that connects the United States to Canada, but you can hike under it.

THE HIKE

After you enter the main entrance to Artpark, go to the upper parking lot called **Niagara 1979**. Yes, you're parking on art! The parking lot is a 43,000-square-foot painting made up of 60 multicolored, two × 364-foot lines. Park in the upper corner, near the metal staircase for the Lower Gorge loop hike. Climb the stairs and turn right to head south on the brick road.

Check out the massive **Omega**, a 110-foot observation deck over the Niagara River created by Owen Morrel. You'll cross Portage Road and see the Upper and Lower Trail entrances to your right. This location is a stop on the Niagara Discovery Shuttle, too.

For the best views, take the #7 Artpark Gorge Trail. This is an easy trail that requires no trail markers. Simply follow the well-worn trail heading south and take in the dramatic **Niagara Escarpment**.

The sediment layers in the gorge walls are easy to spot by the color variations, including Lockport Dolomite (light gray), Rochester Shale (dark gray), and Medina and Queenston Sandstone (red). Tons of these rocks are part of the many rockslides and boulders you'll pass along the trail. The salts from these rocks give the Niagara River its unique green color!

As you approach the **Lewiston-Queenston Bridge**, you'll see a cute picnic spot featuring a beautiful waterfall and small plunge pool that in spring kids play and dip their feet in.

Artpark switchback stairs to lower path

If you continue on the trail past the bridge, you'll see another ephemeral waterfall.

To stay within this 2.5-mile loop, take the stairs that you'll pass on your right down the slope. **Warning: these are presently rough and steep switchback stairs without a railing and are not suitable for everyone.**

Your reward for making it down the stairs is coming to a stunning overlook of the **Niagara Gorge**. As you sit and relax, take in the birds above and below you, gliding on the thermals and hunting for prey in Niagara's abundant water. The Niagara River is a globally significant Important Bird Area (IBA) and is famous for its gulls and migratory birds. For birding information, visit www.birdsontheniagara.org.

Heading back north on the trail, you'll be walking with the current. Several side trails that have been used for decades by anglers will take you to the water's edge. This section of the Niagara River is considered one of the best fishing spots in North America due to the variety, size, and abundance of fish.

Fishing the Niagara is a 12-month season. Depending on the time of the year, you'll see boaters and shore anglers fishing for steelhead, salmon, walleye, smallmouth bass, brown trout, and smelt.

As you near the end of the trail, you'll again see the Omega overlook peering over the Niagara Gorge. Head back to the parking lot or the Discovery Shuttle stop.

PLANNING YOUR VISIT

If you go for a wonderful **summer** stroll, the trails will be busier at this time of year. The noise from the boats and helicopters can be annoying during the day. If you're seeking a quieter experience, go in the early morning when there are only anglers on the trail. The absolute best time to hike the gorge is in the **fall**. The combination of yellow, red, and green leaves along the cliffs of the gorge, with the turquoise-green water passing by, is magical. In **winter and spring**, check for trail closures before going; rockslides are common this time of year.

Artpark ephemeral waterfall

HIKING DATES

HIKING NOTES

DeVeaux Woods
old-growth tree

4

DeVeaux Woods Ancient Forest and the Lonely Grave

LOCATION: Deveaux Woods State Park,
Niagara Falls, NY
GPS: 43.119230, –79.060586

FEATURES: This 51-acre pocket park has a 10-acre ancient forest tucked inside it! As you walk the forest trails, you are experiencing the same scene that early European explorers such as Hennepin and Champlain did in the 1600s. An unusual feature is the single gravestone tucked next to a trail.

DISTANCE: 1.25 mile/loop
LEVEL OF DIFFICULTY: Easy
USAGE ICONS:

BEST SEASONS:

TRAIL MAP: https://bit.ly/SPWNY7
MANAGED BY: New York State Parks

Abandoned DeVeaux College for Orphans and Destitute Children

Walk among 10 acres of towering, massive red oaks, white oaks, and black oaks that are 225 to 280 years old!

UNIQUE FEATURES

Ancient forest: An ancient forest is ripe for exploration in this city pocket park.

The lonely grave: A single grave, tucked alongside a grassy trail, is a curious and unexpected find.

A BRIEF HISTORY

This property was deeded to Judge Samuel DeVeaux in 1852 for the purpose of creating the DeVeaux College for Orphans and Destitute Children. The 51-acre campus housed a dozen buildings and three residences. The imposing Van Rensselaer Hall building still dominates the landscape. In 1972, DeVeaux College closed, and the property was sold to Niagara University.

For 20 years, Niagara University used the site for college dorms and an art gallery, but when there was no longer a need for the additional space, the university made plans to sell the land to developers.

However, Bruce Kershner, coauthor and then-member of the Western New York Old Growth Forest Survey, had been conducting research on the site of old-growth forests, confirming "10 acres of 225–280 yr. towering, massive Red, White, Black Oaks close to the Niagara Gorge, next to Robert Moses Parkway" in the Old Growth Forest Survey of October 2003.

Because of Bruce's efforts and those of many others, instead of the planned commercial development, the land became the 159th New York State Park in May 2000. Bruce's advocacy to protect DeVeaux Woods is legendary.

THE HIKES

Ancient forest hike: Start out by walking on the paved path that goes past the Park Office building. Don't be thrown by the prominent "Do Not Enter" signs; they're aimed at cars, not hikers. The entrance is to the right and has educational signage on old-growth forests.

This is a level, easy-paced, 0.40-mile, out-and-back hike. As you meander the wood-chipped path, you'll pass giant red oaks, white oaks, and black oaks that are massive in girth and reach high into the sky. Look past the path, deep into the woods, to see even more of these monstrous, old-growth trees. This is a rare glimpse into how the Niagara region looked 300-plus years ago, before European settlement.

Lonely Grave hike: Cross the paved trail to the other side, and follow the intertwining paths of mown grass. Continue to walk north (toward the gorge). The forest is not as dense on this side of the park. As you

Find the lonely grave of Eliza A. Keig.

peek deeper into the woods, there are more stands of old-growth trees, just not as dense and undisturbed as the Ancient Forest trail.

The **Lonely Grave** is tucked slightly off the trail with a small footpath providing entrance. The gravestone is marked with "Eliza A. Keig, Born Apr. 18, 1843, Died Dec. 7, 1865. In perfect peace." and is surrounded by massive old trees. When we were there, amulets had been placed on the grave, as well as stones to define the burial area.

Quite a bit of research and writing has been done about Eliza that you can find online by searching for "DeVeaux Woods Grave."

PLANNING YOUR VISIT

Walking the trails in **summer**, you'll see the leafed-out and mighty old-growth oaks, as well as a variety of wildflowers, such as orange, bulbous jack-in-the-pulpit and broadleaf enchanter's nightshade. If you have little ones with you, the playground is fantastic. Four-legged friends can play in the new bark park, too!

The park is used as an outdoor laboratory by Niagara University, and you may see students doing field study projects in the **fall**. This is an easy, short stroll to take in the autumn colors on the leaves and grasses.

DeVeaux Woods is a **winter** playground. The trails can be used for easy snowshoeing and cross-country skiing, and there is an ice rink for skating, too.

Early spring is perhaps the best time to appreciate the ancient forest. You can peer upward without the leaf canopy and fully appreciate the girth and height of these giants. This is the quietest time to stroll through the woods.

HIKING DATES

____

____

____

HIKING NOTES

____

____

____

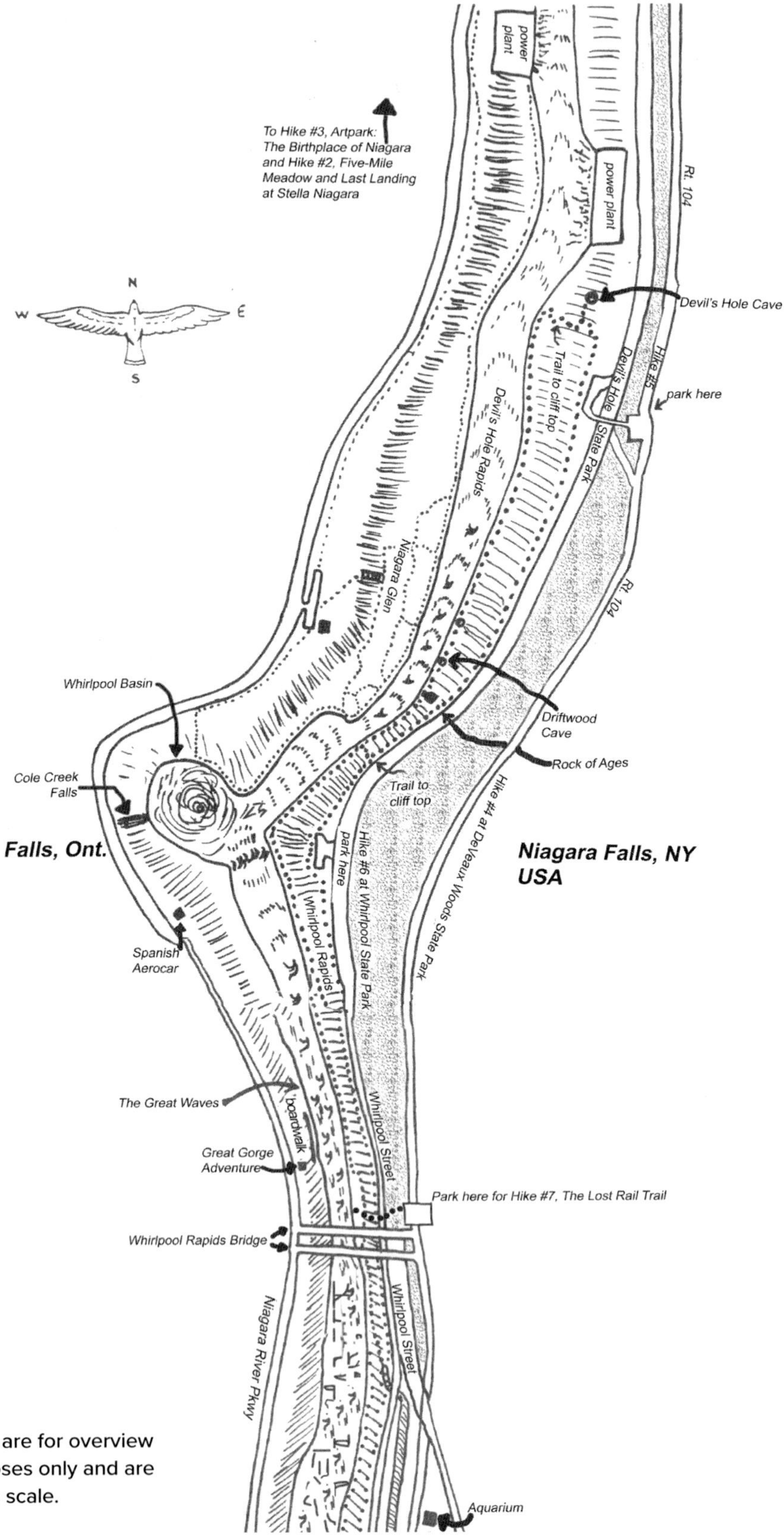

Maps are for overview purposes only and are not to scale.

5

Devil's Hole and the Cave of the Evil Spirit

LOCATION: Devil's Hole State Park, Niagara Falls, NY
GPS: 43.133270, –79.047338

FEATURES: This dramatic hike into the lower Niagara Gorge plummets 315 feet in from rim to river. Descend the winding stone staircase while peering into the depth of Devil's Hole Gulch, a steep ravine that is the site of the 1763 massacre of British soldiers by Seneca warriors. Peek into "secret" caves, including one with its own waterfall hidden inside!

DISTANCE: 2.5 miles, round trip (add Whirlpool State Park for an additional 2.5 miles)
LEVEL OF DIFFICULTY: Moderate
USAGE ICONS:

BEST SEASONS:

TRAIL MAP: https://bit.ly/SPWNY_NFGORGE
MANAGED BY: New York State Parks

Peek inside the Cave of the Evil Spirit at Devil's Hole.

This world-class hike includes secret caves you can explore.

UNIQUE FEATURES

Niagara Gorge: Carved out more than 12,000 years ago, Niagara Falls formed this area of the Niagara Gorge. The 315-foot-deep gorge is still wild and a remarkable sight to behold. The rugged cliffside gives you a glimpse of what a dry Niagara Falls looks like.

Devil's Hole Gulch: This is the site of the 1763 massacre of an estimated 143 British soldiers by Seneca warriors. Their bodies, most of them scalped, along with their wagons and animals, were found at the bottom of the gulch. Accounts of the scene recall the small tributary at Devil's Hole ran red with blood, giving the creek the name of Bloody Run.

Cave of the Evil Spirit: Also known as Devil's Hole Cave, this 50-foot-deep cavern is located on a side trail, halfway down the staircase. Its name comes from a traditional Seneca Indian story, handed down for generations, that an evil spirit was trapped in the cave when this was the site of Niagara Falls. When Niagara Falls moved further south, the evil spirit was set free. French explorer René-Robert Cavelier, de La Salle, despite being counseled by his Seneca guide not to enter the cave, ventured in with his men. His expeditions were later marred by mishaps, followed by his murder in 1687.

Devil's Hole Rapids: This series of churning, 7- to 12-foot-high rapids in the Niagara River has only one other comparable site upstream, at the Whirlpool rapids.

Rock of Ages: This giant, vertical, 30-foot megalith (giant boulder) is perched on the river's edge.

Driftwood Cave: This remarkable cave has a waterfall inside it! This boulder cave is 80 feet long and two to five feet high in sections. The main entrance is 20 feet wide and is visible and accessible from the trail. The cave always has an ample supply of driftwood. Maybe it's deposited by high water during winter storms, but it's just as likely to be brought by the same folks who made the illegal firepit. Ironically, the waterfall that drips from an opening at the top keeps the cave too damp for fires.

THE HIKE

From the parking lot, head to the gorge rim, and walk north (right) toward the view of the Niagara Power Project. Take in the spectacular view of the Niagara River. From this height, it seems deceivingly peaceful.

The Devil's Hole Trail decreases in elevation at the rim as you pass the Comfort Station. As the trail turns left, take the stone stairs to descend into a semicircular amphitheater with its stairs hugging the cliff walls.

Although it's tempting to want to get this part of the hike over quickly, consider the geological history as you walk down. To your left is Devil's Hole, the remnant of the dried-up Bloody Run waterfall which drained glacial Lake Tonawanda. When that lake dried up, it left the unfinished gorge you see today. The ancient Bloody Run waterfall is now a tiny trickle after heavy rains.

Count the steps as you descend. After step 88, a side trail will emerge at the right. Take this to ascend to the **Cave of the Evil Spirit**. The stairs are crumbled and damaged. Don't attempt this in wet weather! The trail ends at a small, flat area in front of the eight-foot cave opening.

Giant, 30-foot Rock of Ages at river's edge

If you choose to enter the cave, be careful of broken glass. The depth is about 50 feet. It used to go farther back into other rooms, but rockslides blocked access years ago.

Head back onto the main stairs descending into the gorge. Once at the bottom of the trail, turn left upstream. You'll pass along the bottom of **Devil's Hole Gulch**, where some still claim to hear the spirits. A half-mile later, you'll reach the striking **Rock of Ages** that was once part of the cliff face directly above you. (Did we mention watch for rockslides?)

To find **Driftwood Cave**, you have to walk downstream 100 steps from the Rock of Ages. The entrance is visible from the trail, but it's often overlooked. If you go inside, go all the way toward the sound of water dripping. Stop and look up! Not only is there a waterfall, but also a chimney going up at the back at a 60-degree angle with a tiny dot of light way, way up at the top. If the cave walls could talk, what stories could it tell? What did the first inhabitants of this region use this cave for?

Continue left toward the whirlpool, and you'll see occasional crevices and alcoves a few feet across and deep in the rock wall. There are rumors of additional caves in this area, but we didn't see any that seemed safe to explore.

As you hike on flat sections of the trail, you occasionally get a peek at the foundation of the Great Gorge Route Railroad that hugged the shoreline and operated until 1935, when a massive rockslide closed it forever (yep, rockslides again—it's a theme!).

Note the imposing, 300-foot-high cliffs surrounding you and recall how calm the Niagara River looked from above. Now, standing next to the violent Devil's Hole Rapids with its swift and circular currents, "calm" isn't the right adjective to use anymore.

The mighty **Niagara River** drains the world's greatest freshwater lake system, and it's flowing through this narrow gorge right before your eyes! This truly is one of the most awe-inspiring hikes in North America.

As you come to a picnic area with a few stone tables, the Devil's Hole Trail ends. You can choose to backtrack the way you came, hike up the Whirlpool Park steps, or if you want to continue your hike, see Chapter 6 to follow the trail: **Whirlpool Rapids and the Basin**.

PLANNING YOUR VISIT

Summer is busy! Local hikers and tourists take advantage of this beautiful trail system that connects to six other trails. **Fall** is by far the best time to experience the gorge. The fall colors are spectacular with yellow birches, red maples, and orange oaks. **Late fall** and **spring** are ideal for bird-watching. In April and May, the salmon are running, and you'll see fishermen trying their luck. **Winter** is not advised; rockslides, ice, and poor conditions make this trail very dangerous.

> **HIKING TIP:** If you're exploring the caves, bring a headlamp and appropriate gear.

HIKING DATES

HIKING NOTES

Descend 500 stone steps
on the Whirlpool Trail.

6

Whirlpool Rapids, the Great Waves, and the Basin

LOCATION: Whirlpool State Park, Niagara Falls, NY
GPS: 43.120145, –79.064091

FEATURES: One of the most exciting hikes on the East Coast features the largest series of standing waves in North America. Standing near the Great Waves, all other sound is blocked while you hear and feel the pounding, 20-foot-tall walls of water violently move past you.

DISTANCE: 2.5 miles, round trip (add Devil's Hole State Park for an additional 2.5 miles)
LEVEL OF DIFFICULTY: Moderate to difficult
USAGE ICONS:

BEST SEASONS:

TRAIL MAP: https://bit.ly/SPWNY_NFGORGE; refer to the chapter map for additional details
MANAGED BY: New York State Parks

You'll find the largest series of standing freshwater waves in North America on this hike.

UNIQUE FEATURES

Niagara Gorge: This seven-mile stretch of the Niagara Gorge is 250 feet deep. Looking up at the rock wall, you can see the layers of limestone, shale, sandstone, and dolostone that compose the distinct layers of Niagara Falls and the Niagara Gorge.

The dolostone, an altered, hardened form of limestone, is the caprock that the water flows over and is more resistant to erosion. However, the lower layers of shale and sandstone are prone to erosion, which is evident by the precarious and intimidating limestone rock overhangs. These overhangs break off during the freeze/thaw cycle and are the cause of annual spring rockslides. **BEWARE:** Rockslides are real, and the trail can be closed or blocked in the winter and spring due to them.

Whirlpool Basin: The Niagara River takes a sharp, right-angled turn at this large, round basin. Dangerous whirling currents carry floating objects "round and round" and often suck them underwater and then dramatically shoot them up into the air! Hikers have reported giant trees and barrel drums popping out unexpectedly.

Whirlpool Rapids: These world-class phenomena are the largest standing freshwater waves in North America. The standing **Great Waves** can reach 12 to 20 feet high, curl under themselves, crash, shift, and churn with dangerous and awesome power. The quarter-mile trail section is an unreal sight and sound. If you lie on the old train platform, you can feel the vibration of the waves. The Great Waves are caused by the huge volume of water flowing from four of the five Great Lakes being forced through this narrow channel towards Lake Ontario.

Titan Rock: This colossal, 40-foot-high boulder fell from the Niagara Escarpment above and stopped on the edge of the river, slightly overhanging it. It's been a popular photo spot for locals and tourists as far back as the 1800s.

THE HIKE

Starting from Whirlpool State Park, follow the Gorge Rim Trail to the right (north) until you reach the stone staircase. Luckily, the 500 stone steps were recently repointed and are much more stable than in past years. The descent is fairly quick, and you'll come out to the main trail where stone picnic benches await to give you a chance to catch your breath. (Alternatively, you can start at Devil's Hole State Park and continue walking past the stone picnic tables.)

Whirlpool trail

Great Gorge train platform, used from 1895-1935

Head upstream toward the Spanish Aero Car that spans the Whirlpool Basin. Check out one of the side paths that lead to the water's edge. **Be careful because the rocks can be slippery, and NEVER go in the water.** As you get closer to the Spanish Aero Car, you'll ascend a few rockslide areas and come out onto Whirlpool Point. This flat, rocky point juts out into the **Whirlpool Basin** and is a favorite spot for picnicking, sunning, and enjoying the views on warm, sunny days.

The Whirlpool Basin often has an array of odd debris floating in the water—including entire trees, storage drums, and miscellaneous boating gear. Over on the Canadian shoreline, try to spot the lonely blue boat and imagine what mishap caused it to be stranded in such a dangerous spot.

The trail becomes narrower and steeper after you go past the Whirlpool Basin, but the effort is worth it for those who are able. You'll pass **Titan Rock**, the 40-foot-high boulder that is an age-old tourist spot. Soon, you'll start seeing the end of the Great Waves. Trek on! As you look to the Canadian side, the **Great Waves** are in front of the Great Gorge Adventure platform.

You'll come to the old Great Gorge Train platform. This is a perfect spot to have a full sensory experience of the Great Waves. Sit on the platform and feel the vibration while your eyes take it in, your ears ring, and you're overwhelmed by the smell of aerated water. Imagine the intensity of these waves if there were no hydroelectric water diversions!

The trail is closed at this point and is not yet connected to the Great Gorge Rail Trail. New York State Parks will make this connection in the future, but until then, hike back the way you came.

PLANNING YOUR VISIT

This is the most popular hike in the Niagara Gorge Trail System. It's not unusual to see hundreds of hikers during a warm **summer** day. If you want solitude, join the anglers for a sunrise hike. By far, the best time to experience the gorge is **fall.** The autumn colors are spectacular: yellow birches, red maples, and orange oaks. Birdwatching is best in the late fall. Hiking in **winter and early spring** is not advised; rockslides, ice, and poor conditions make this trail very dangerous and often closed. **Late spring,** April/May, is great for birdwatching. The debris in the Whirlpool Basin is heaviest in the spring. Bring a walking stick and wear good hiking shoes.

HIKING DATES

____

____

____

HIKING NOTES

____

____

____

The lost rail trail steps

7

The Lost Rail Trail of Niagara

LOCATION: Gorge Stairs Trailhead parking lot on Whirlpool Street, opposite Ontario Avenue intersection, Niagara Falls, NY

GPS: 43.108538, –79.056145

FEATURES: The most gorgeous hike you'll ever experience! Follow the long-forgotten path of the scenic 1895 Niagara Gorge Belt Line railroad and enjoy picture-postcard-perfect views of Niagara Falls, the Niagara River, and the surrounding gorge.

DISTANCE: 4 miles/loop

LEVEL OF DIFFICULTY: Moderate to difficult

USAGE ICONS:

BEST SEASONS:

TRAIL MAP: https://bit.ly/SPWNY_NFGORGE; refer to the chapter map for additional details

MANAGED BY: New York State Parks

Discover Niagara Falls framed by the Rainbow Bridge along the Lost Rail Trail.

With Niagara Falls framed by the Rainbow Bridge, the view is picture-postcard perfect.

A BRIEF HISTORY

The Great Gorge Trip: From 1895 to 1935, the 20-mile scenic Great Gorge Trip was an electric railroad that started from Niagara Falls and ran along the base of the Niagara Gorge into Lewiston and crossed the Niagara River to run along the top of the gorge on the Canadian side.

For just $1, tourists could hop on and off the railcars, with cars running every 15 minutes during summer. This widely popular tourist attraction was forced to close in 1935 after a 5,000-ton rockslide destroyed 200 feet of track north of the Whirlpool Bridge.

At the time of its closure, more than 13 million passengers had ridden on the Great Gorge Route and experienced the magnificent view of the Whirlpool Rapids. This nature trail and a few exposed railbeds and brick supports are the only remains.

UNIQUE FEATURES

Suspension Bridge: A quick little side hike will take you to the ruins of the 1855 Niagara Falls Railway Suspension Bridge. This will also be a future hiking trail connected to the remainder of the Niagara Gorge trail system.

A giant hole: High on the rock cliff wall, closer to the Schoellkopf Power Station ruins, there is a human-sized hole in the rock face that few notice. It's a bizarre relic from bygone industrial times.

The $1,000,000 view: As you hike south toward the majestic cataract, your senses will become overwhelmed by the sound of water from the four great lakes crashing over Niagara and plunging 167 feet into the Niagara River. The sound becomes deafening the closer you get, and the view is **picture-postcard perfect**, with Niagara Falls framed by the Rainbow Bridge.

Schoellkopf Power Station ruins: This hydroelectric power plant collapsed into the gorge in 1956. At the base of the ruins, there are interpretive displays describing the power project's impact and eventual collapse.

Get a free ride: At the base of the Schoellkopf Power Station is an elevator, for a free ride back up to the top of the gorge.

Free elevator ride down to the base of the Schoellkopf Power Station

The Lost Rail Trail along the Niagara Gorge

THE HIKE

Take this recommended route! You'll hike into the view and sounds of Niagara Falls and get the option of a free elevator ride back to the top of the gorge. The trailhead is at the abandoned 1855 Suspension Bridge ruins.

Begin your hike by taking the 100-plus stone steps that descend 175 feet into the Niagara Gorge. If the stairs have you reconsidering this hike, it gets more challenging as the trail gets closer to the Schoellkopf power station. *This is a hike, not a walk. Wear good shoes and bring a day pack!* Use good judgment when deciding if you should bring children and pets.

When you reach the bottom of the stairs, take a quick side trip to the north toward the **Suspension Bridge**. This little 10-minute jaunt is picture-worthy as you stand under the abutments of the old Suspension Bridge. The trail becomes impassable in this direction, so you'll be forced to turn around.

The first mile of this trail is easy and flat. It follows the old train line and offers fantastic views of the rock layers under the Falls. Stop and look up at the stone cliffs made of layers of resistant dolostone that cap Niagara Falls, along with the weaker layers of limestone below, carved away as the falls migrated upstream.

About a mile into the trail, it divides into upper and lower paths. Take the lower path, and you'll discover metal stairs that steeply descend to the river level. Turn around and look up at the cliff to see a **giant, human-sized hole** in the rock wall above you! You might not have noticed it while on the trail, but with a little distance, you can see this massive carved relic from bygone days of harnessing the hydropower of the Niagara River's waters.

From your vantage on the metal stairs, you can see the modern, brutalist-style sewage plant tucked into the side of the gorge. At the base of the stairs is an active, water-level gauge station operated by the National Oceanic and Atmospheric Administration. Behave . . . you're under live video surveillance!

Look out at the water, which is smooth and deceptive. The current runs swiftly from the plunge pool of Niagara to where the Whirlpool Rapids start, two miles downstream. You can see the mini-vortices swirling in the river below. This a tame preview of how turbulent the water becomes.

Find the giant, human-size hole in the cliff face above you.

As you resume your hike upriver, the trail quickly lowers its elevation through some switchbacks to get you closer to river level. There are **curious and odd items** along the trail, including a few rusting cars, old rail tracks, and a few shopping carts. Unfortunate past dumping practices have left this debris to slowly rust away into the hillside.

The trail becomes less groomed and wilder as you approach the end, which is rocky, rooty, and winding. Just as you start to see the ruins of the **old Schoellkopf Power Station**, the trail turns into a massive concrete pad where the Maid of the Mist boats are stored.

Look up to see the Schoellkopf Power Station Museum, which is on the National Register of Historic Places. The museum is built on the ruins of the hydroelectric power plant that collapsed into the gorge in 1956. At the base of the monumental stone tower, you'll find the **free elevator** to take you back to street level.

PLANNING YOUR VISIT

Summer is the most popular time to enjoy Niagara Falls and the beautiful park system. The trails will be busy, but there are still quiet spots to sit and take in nature. The ferns and natural fauna hanging from the cliff crevices are a beautiful sight. The air is cooler near the water, and the gorge acts as a natural wind block. The trails are mostly shaded and provide a nice escape on a hot, summer day.

Fall is the best time to go as it's quieter, and the gorge is afire with beautiful autumn colors! In October, hundreds of fishermen can be found casting their lines into the water for trout, salmon, and bass. In the fall and spring, thousands of migratory birds fly overhead, including gulls, raptors, and geese, which can be seen both migrating and hunting for a quick meal.

The lower Niagara Gorge Trails are closed **mid-November to April** due to dangerous conditions. Bring a hiking pole on this trip, and wear good hiking boots.

HIKING DATES

HIKING NOTES

Ruins from the collapsed Schoellkopf Power Station

Discover secret overlooks tucked into wooded trails along the trail.

8

The Portage: Niagara Gorge Upper Rim Trail

LOCATION: Niagara Falls State Park, NY
GPS: 43.085825, –79.068565

FEATURES: Follow the 7-mile portage that native peoples and early settlers took to bypass the unnavigable rapids and Niagara Falls. Today, this is an easy, scenic, and gorgeous hike with stunning overlooks and vistas.

DISTANCE: 6.5 miles, one way. Shorter segments are available by starting and stopping at Devil's Hole State Park, Whirlpool State Park, the Great Gorge Rail Trail, and Niagara Falls State Park.
LEVEL OF DIFFICULTY: Easy
USAGE ICONS:

BEST SEASONS:

TRAIL MAP: https://bit.ly/SPWNY_NFGORGE; refer to the chapter map for additional details.
MANAGED BY: New York State Parks

Along the upper trail, there is a secret spot where you can hear Niagara Falls in your left ear and the Whirlpool Rapids in your right ear.

UNIQUE FEATURES

Prospect Point (Niagara Falls, USA): Adjacent to the **American Falls,** this is the best view on the American side. You're surrounded by the mist while hearing the river crash 167 feet over the falls. The actual plunge, including the water depth, is 185 feet! It was here that Nik Wallenda began his high-wire walk over Niagara Falls in 2012, being the first daredevil to high-wire directly over the brink of the falls.

Rainbow Bridge Lovelocks: Most visitors go over the Rainbow Bridge, but this hike goes under the 1941 bridge to see the hundreds of "love locks" attached to the chain-link fence. Left by lovers from all over the world, this tradition of attaching a padlock (with your love's name on it) to a fence over a bridge dates back more than 100 years.

Schoellkopf Overlook and Elevator: A free and quick ride in the Schoellkopf elevator takes you to the base of the Niagara Gorge, where you can see ruins of the Schoellkopf Power Station. Built between 1905 and 1924, this was the largest hydroelectric power plant in the world. Disaster struck in 1956, when the power station was destroyed in a catastrophic collapse.

Love locks tucked under the Rainbow Bridge

Suspension Bridge Overlook (a special little secret spot): Along the walking trail, between Linwood Avenue and Division Street, is a little, hidden dirt trail that leads to a rock seat that overlooks the Suspension Bridge. Not only is this a wonderful sight, but it also features a special sound heard nowhere else on earth (GPS below in the hike description). Covering one ear and then the other, you'll hear two entirely different, world-class, rushing water features at this auditory halfway point.

Great Gorge Rail Trail: Positioned next to the Suspension Bridge abutment and in Freedom Plaza, you'll find the newest stone steps that descend into the Niagara Gorge. This trail follows the route upstream that the Niagara Gorge Railway Trolley took its passengers on from 1895 to 1935. For details on the lower tier hike, see Chapter 7, *The Lost Rail Trail of Niagara*.

DiCamillo's Bakery: How can there be so much goodness in one bakery? A Niagara Falls tradition since 1920, you can't get this close and not stop in for the fresh-baked rolls, pastries, and biscotti that are shipped all over the world. There's ice cream and Italian ice too!

Whirlpool State Park: This park provides beautiful scenic vistas of the Whirlpool Basin and rapids. It also serves as a nice halfway point to stop and picnic before continuing on. For details on Whirlpool State Park's lower trail, see Chapter 6, *Whirlpool Rapids, the Great Waves, and the Basin*.

Devil's Hole State Park: This park is the site of the 1763 massacre of British soldiers by Seneca warriors, as well as the geological formation called Devil's Hole Gulch. You can see this formation from the upper rim trail. For details on Devil's Hole State Park's lower trail, see Chapter 5, *Devil's Hole and the Cave of the Evil Spirit*.

Robert Moses Power Plant: Producing 2.6 million kilowatts of electricity, the Niagara Falls Power Plant turbines cycle through 748,000 gallons of water per second before releasing the water into Lake Ontario. Learn more at the Power Vista visitors center, and go out on the observation deck for an amazing panoramic view of the Niagara Gorge.

Hidden overlook gives a bird's-eye view of the Suspension bridge and Whirlpool Rapids.

THE HIKE

This is an easy, paved, and scenic walk (or bike ride) that provides frequent stops at the numerous gorge overlook sites to get a bird's-eye view of the Niagara Gorge system. What's wonderful about this hike is that you can start at several different trailheads, depending on your location and ambition.

> **LOCAL TIP:** If you can start out at Whirlpool State Park and walk toward the falls, you'll have the view in front of you.

Otherwise, start out at **Prospect Point**, the location where the **American Falls** crashes into the lower Niagara River. This vantage gives the best view on the American side of the **Horseshoe Falls**. For a modest price, you can take the **Observation Deck** elevator down to

the base of the American Falls for the thunderous experience. Here, surrounded by the mist, you hear the Niagara River throw itself 167 feet over the falls.

From Prospect Point, head right (north) on the well-marked **#2 Niagara Gorge Rim Trail** with the **Rainbow Bridge** as your waymarker. Take the path that crosses under the bridge for a panoramic view of Niagara Falls that few get to see from this location and to appreciate the **hundreds of love locks** attached to the security fence under the bridge. And remember to always be smiling, because you're on camera at this highly secure international border crossing.

Continuing right (north), you'll come to the site of the **Schoellkopf Overlook and Elevator**. You can go out on the overlook rail to get the upper view of the power plant ruins, but the most impressive view is from the base of the elevator, looking up. The base is paved and fully accessible for wheeled visitors. There are interpretive signs, an up-close view of the lower Niagara River, and trail access to the American Falls and Great Gorge Railway Trails.

Back on the upper trail, just behind the aquarium, is one of the first of many **"secret" overlooks** that locals have known about for years. With the recent park renovations, these hidden overlooks are less daunting to visitors, but still may have a few beer bottles and old firepits from late-night parties. You'll pass a handful more of these on your way to the **Suspension Bridge**.

The park becomes quieter as you leave the downtown hotel area, taking on a more natural setting with tall grasses, seasonal wildflowers, and large old cherry and oak trees. Peek over the gorge rail and look for the **ancient white cedar trees** that cling to the cliff walls. These could be the oldest living trees in the northeastern United States! In a March 4, 2001, *Buffalo News* article, coauthor Bruce Kershner, then chairman of the Western New York Old Growth Forest Survey, stated that "they are conservatively at least 500 to 800 years old."

As the sound of Niagara Falls starts to fade, the Suspension Bridge is your new waymarker. It's along this section that you'll find the secret spot (GPS**:** 43.104504, –79.05593) on another hidden overlook that frames your view of the Suspension Bridge. This is the spot where you can hear both Niagara Falls and the Whirlpool Rapids.

Now is a good stopping place to relax. Take a short side trip to a local favorite, **DiCamillo's Bakery**, located on Linwood Avenue. The street intersects with the park here, and there's outdoor seating in nice weather where you can enjoy coffee, ice cream, or biscotti from this 100-year-old, world-famous bakery.

Continuing on the upper trail, you'll pass by the ruins of the old Suspension Bridge, and the staircase down to the **Lost Rail Trail Hike** found in Chapter 7. On the right of the trail is the **Niagara Falls Underground Railroad Heritage Center**, colocated with the International Amtrak Station. This is a fantastic location to take in the important role abolitionists and the people of Niagara Falls had in facilitating freedom for enslaved peoples.

Whirlpool Rapids and Great Waves view from the upper trail

Between the Suspension Bridge and **Whirlpool State Park** is the site of the **Great Waves**. These are the 12- to 20-foot-high **Whirlpool Rapids!** Even from the rim trail, you can hear the roiling below and see the angry white water waves. As you begin to veer left, the **Spanish Aero Car** high above you will be your visual waymarker. Start looking down to see **Whirlpool Point**, which juts out into the Whirlpool Basin. Soon, you'll pass Whirlpool State Park and the stairs to the Whirlpool Rapids, Great Waves, and the Basin hike described in Chapter 6.

Bypassing the stairs and continuing north to **Devil's Hole State Park**, you'll walk through a quiet, wooded trail and watch the gorge's deceivingly calm swirling waters. The beautiful blue-green color comes from the mineral deposits found in the pulverized rocks and salts. This rock flour is made from limestone, shales, and sandstones found in the layers under the falls.

Looking up at the Schoellkopf Power Plant ruins and landing

At Devil's Hole, you'll get a sweeping downstream view of the **Niagara Falls Power Project**. In spring, summer, and fall, you'll see dozens of fishing boats near the outtakes of the Power Project, as this is one of the best fishing spots in the Niagara River for steelhead and king salmon. Because of this, you'll also see an abundance of migratory birds feeding on the bounty below.

The trail takes you past the stone stairs that plunge into Devil's Hole, the site of the 1763 massacre of British soldiers by Seneca warriors as well as the geological formations of **Devil's Hole Gulch**. To learn more about what's on the lower trail, read Chapter 5, Devil's Hole and the Cave of the Evil Spirit.

The last stop on this walking or biking trip is the **Niagara Falls Power Project**. Go out on the observation deck of the Power Vista and take in the sweeping views all the way into Lewiston and Queenston, Ontario (Canada), across the river.

This trail continues down the Niagara Escarpment into Lewiston and meets up with the **Artpark Gorge Trail**. See Chapter 3, The Birthplace of Niagara: Niagara Escarpment Trails at Artpark, to learn more. If you walked, you can take the Niagara Discovery Shuttle back (in season), or you can return the way you came.

For the really active souls out there: a recommended full-day itinerary is to hike the *lower trail* from Artpark to Niagara Falls (recreating the 7.2-mile portage the native peoples and early settlers took to bypass the falls), and then hike the *upper trail* back to your vehicle. This is a 15-mile-round-trip route.

PLANNING YOUR VISIT

Summer is the most popular time to enjoy Niagara Falls and the beautiful park system. The trails will be busy in some places and quiet in others. **Fall** is the best time to go. It's a little quieter, and the cliffs are adorned in beautiful autumn colors. In the skies overhead, you'll see gulls, raptors, and geese both migrating and hunting for a quick meal.

Early and late spring are two of the prettiest times to enjoy the wildflowers along the trail system. You may luck out and see thousands of migrating birds, including gulls, vultures, loons, swans, grebes, bald eagles, and peregrine falcons. Although the trail is open in the **winter**, it can be windy and cold this time of year.

HIKING DATES

____

____

____

HIKING NOTES

____

____

____

Secret hiding spots inside ancient trees at Reinstein Woods

9

The Ancient Forests of Reinstein Woods

LOCATION: 93 Honorine Dr., Cheektowaga, NY
GPS: 42.891490, –78.717764

FEATURES: These old-growth forests predate European settlement. Beech trees with historic carvings date to the mid-1800s.This 292-acre nature preserve features several trails that take you on an easy hike that passes dozens of secluded ponds and wetlands with stunning seasonal flowers and abundant wildlife.

DISTANCE: 2.5 mile/loop
LEVEL OF DIFFICULTY: Easy
USAGE ICONS:

BEST SEASONS:

TRAIL MAP: https://bit.ly/SPWNY9
MANAGED BY: New York State Department of Environmental Conservation and The Friends of Reinstein Woods

A peaceful winter's walk along Frog Pond

Coauthor Bruce Kershner referred to this area as "Buffalo's Backyard Wilderness."

UNIQUE FEATURES

The Nature Preserve "Woods" is divided into three areas:

Intensive use area: You'll find the Nature Education Center and the boardwalk trail to **Lily Pond** here.

Interpretive trails: There are 2.5 miles of public trails. With a bit of looping back and forth between trails, it's closer to three miles. It's on these trails you can find the **historical carvings** and dozens of **old-growth trees**.

Sanctuary: A small portion (approximately one-third) of the **ancient forest** is closed to the public and reserved for maintenance, monitoring, and research activities.

A BRIEF HISTORY

Purchased in 1932, this is the former estate and private nature sanctuary of Dr. Victor Reinstein. Dr. Reinstein acquired much of the undeveloped land in southern Cheektowaga, including a stand of old-growth forest and wetlands, to become his private preserve.

In the 1930s and 1940s, he created dozens of ponds, planted thousands of trees, and carved out a gravel trail system that highlighted the beauty of his preserve. He did all this with the intention of donating the land to the public and for it to be protected in perpetuity. In 1986, after Dr. Reinstein's death, coauthor Bruce Kershner and others worked with New York State to ensure the transfer of the estate, which today is known as the Reinstein Woods State Nature Preserve.

CAN I STILL SEE OLD-GROWTH TREES?

Yes! You can still see **old-growth trees** on the interpretive trails. There are numerous cherry, sugar maple, and beech trees up to five feet in diameter. Some trees have been dated back 200-plus years. Reinstein Woods is one of the largest virgin forests in New York State and one of the only old-growth forests in a metropolitan area in the United States.

Sadly, in 2017, the **Champion Beech tree** that Reinstein Woods was known for was declared dead. This tree, located on the Beech Tree Trail, was the largest forest-grown beech tree in New York State and is recorded on the Big Tree Registry. According to the Friends of Reinstein Woods, it was in decline from natural causes and lived more than 250 years.

THE HIKE

The **Beech Trail** is dedicated in memory of coauthor Bruce Kershner. Not only did Bruce spend hundreds of hours studying Reinstein Woods, but he was also passionate about protecting these trees. For those who want to learn more, read Bruce's history of the Reinstein Nature Preserve, titled *Buffalo's Backyard Wilderness: An Ecological Study of the Reinstein Woods State Nature Preserve.*

As you walk along the trail, ponder the convergence of conservation that has preserved this old-growth forest. You're surrounded by suburbs with houses, roads, and ample representation of modern commercialism. And, yet, in the midst of all this commotion, you're in a tranquil island oasis and habitat for wildlife.

See thousands of shocking pink water lilies in summer bloom.

The **History Trail** features beech trees with carved initials of early settlers dating to the Civil War. There are 75 trees that have historic carvings. Of course, today we call this graffiti at best and vandalism at worst. As you stroll along the History Trail, stop at the Stone House, the Reinsteins' summer home built in 1965 on the shore of Flattail Lake. It's easy to imagine summer picnics, canoeing, and camp games taking place here.

A walk through Reinstein Woods is not complete without appreciating the man-made ponds and marshes that surround you. **Lily Pond and Heron's Pond** are a photographer's and painter's dream in the spring and summer, when they are covered over with "shocking pink" water lilies.

Lilly pond reminds many of the famous Monet painting of water lilies. This is a sensory feast, taking in the incredible and unique sights, smells, and sounds of birds, frogs, flowers, and fauna.

PLANNING YOUR VISIT

Reinstein Woods is beautiful and accessible in all four seasons. **Summer** is a popular time for families to enjoy the trails of the forest and Lily Pond. If you're seeking a tranquil experience, go when the trails open in the morning or an hour before dusk, where you may catch owls, bats, and herons feeding. The autumn color spectacle in the **fall** is fantastic! Enjoy leaf-peeping without leaving the metropolitan Buffalo area. Don't be surprised to see migrating birds feeding and resting in the marsh and ponds areas before moving on to warmer winter residences.

The quiet beauty of the forest in **winter** is an experience everyone should encounter. The variety of activities offered in the winter include hiking, guided tours, snowshoeing, and cross-country skiing. Either bring your own snowshoes and skis, or rent them for a nominal cost at the Nature Education Center.

Spring welcomes the return of the indigo bunting, warblers, herons, and geese, which are all welcome sights in spring. You can witness beavers and turtles becoming active again. This is one of the few spring hikes that isn't a mud pit, due to the elevated, gravel-lined trails.

HIKING DATES

HIKING NOTES

Not-so-secret Eternal Flames Falls at Shale Creek Gorge

10

Eternal Flames Falls and Shale Creek Gorge

LOCATION: Chestnut Ridge Park, Chestnut Ridge Rd., Orchard Park, NY

GPS: 42.701947, –78.747888

FEATURES: Hike to the bottom of this 30-foot-high waterfall through a serene, wooded gorge, and experience the unique feature that made the 1994 *Secret Places of Western New York and Southern Ontario* book famous.

DISTANCE: 1 mile/in-and-out

LEVEL OF DIFFICULTY: Moderate

USAGE ICONS:

BEST SEASONS:

TRAIL MAP: https://bit.ly/SPWNY-10

MANAGED BY: Erie County Parks, Recreation, and Forestry, Erie County, New York

Light the Eternal Flame

See the natural gas flames that jut out of a grotto three to nine inches and are washed over by the cascading waterfall.

UNIQUE FEATURES

Shale Creek Preserve: The southern part of Chestnut Ridge Park has many trails through shaded hemlock, maple, and pine forests, including the Eternal Flames Trail, Boy Scout Trail, Orienteering Trail, and Seufert Trail (the original Eternal Flames Trail).

Shale Creek Gorge: This 150-foot-deep ravine contains the Eternal Flames Trail and the Eternal Flames Falls.

Eternal Flames Falls: This 30-foot-high waterfall cascades over two steps of layered shale in an exquisitely scenic and graceful manner. At the base, and behind the waterfall, is the small grotto where the flame juts out from the rock, protecting the flame and creating a surreal natural wonder.

The Eternal Flame: Natural gas jets, which can vary from three to nine inches long based on natural pressure changes, cause a flame to flare out from the base of the grotto. At dusk, this creates an eerie flickering light from a distance.

Fun flame facts: In 2013, geologists from the National Institute of Geophysics and Volcanology of Italy and Indiana University Bloomington studied the flame at Eternal Flames Falls and found that the Rhinestreet Shale 1,300 feet below the surface is the source of the natural gas for the flame. The gas is a mixture of methane, ethane, and propane, with methane being the dominant gas. It reaches the surface through cracks associated with faulting caused by tectonic activity.

With the varying gas pressure, the flame can sometimes get extinguished. If you arrive and the flame is out, simply light it by flicking a lighter at the bottom of the wall of the grotto. Don't worry, the flame is tame and will not "blow up" like a gas grill, and the rock temperatures are as mild as a cup of warm tea. The most dangerous part of lighting the flame is keeping your balance on the slippery rocks.

THE HIKE

Starting at the Chestnut Ridge Road parking lot, there is a large trailhead sign with trail maps. You quickly see the first flame-logo trail markers as the gravel turns to earth and you begin descending into a wooded grove of hemlocks, maples, and pines.

Follow the well-marked trail, extensively reconstructed in 2023, as it slowly zigzags and descends into the **Shale Creek Gorge**. After you reach the bottom where Shale Creek is, turn left and follow the creek to the waterfall. You can hike on the side of the creek, or for the more adventurous (and those with water shoes), hike right in the creek.

This is a leisurely hike to savor and enjoy; be sure to take in the old, large hemlocks with gnarly roots that line the creek bed. During the late spring and summer, you can see tadpoles and small schools of guppies in the creek.

As you get closer to your final destination of the **Eternal Flames Falls**, look up at the impressive 150-foot-high shale walls that consist of Hanover Shale from the Upper Devonian period, believed to be 375 million years old. The Hanover Shale is a cool, greenish-gray rock with some black bands.

As you approach the **Eternal Flame**, marvel and take in the white noise of the waterfall and the mysteriousness of the forest. Some visitors feel a spiritual reverence at this remarkable spot.

Turn back and head out the creek trail the way you came in.

PLANNING YOUR VISIT

The best way for first-time visitors to hike the trail is during the day, but the best view of the flame is at dusk, and the park is closed from dusk to dawn. A tip from coauthor Bruce Kershner is to first go during the day, memorize the route, and then plan your return visit one hour before sunset. This will give you enough time to hike in, sit for a while, marvel at the waterfall and the quietness of the evening forest, and then quickly hike out, equipped with your headlamp. Check your batteries before you go!

Summer is the most high-traffic time of the year. The trail is heavily hiked, especially during the weekends. Even with the crowds, it's still a rewarding hike to enjoy on a hot summer day. Bring your splash shoes and hike in the creek during low-water levels, but use caution on the slippery, algae-covered rocks!

Enjoy the red and yellow maple canopy with a dappling of green hemlocks and pines along the hike. The crisp **fall** air, coupled with fewer crowds, brings this hike closer to the "secret place" spirit of this book.

In **winter**, the Eternal Flame becomes a truly magical experience, with flames leaping out of the grotto behind the ice-covered waterfall. An alternative hike is to experience the view of the waterfall from above. To do this, take the Boy Scout Trail to the end (2.5 miles), and you can peer over the edge of Shale Creek Gorge to see the Flame below, where it gives the appearance of a small campfire tucked under the ice and grotto formation. Check water levels before attempting a **spring** hike. Rain and snow melt can make this hike too treacherous.

HIKING DATES

HIKING NOTES

Eternal Flame trail marker

Towering sand dunes and ancient oaks at Wendt Beach

11

Sister Beaches of Erie: The Bluffs, Ancient Trees, Sunken Boardwalks, and Ice Volcanoes

LOCATION: Bennett Beach and Wendt Beach parks, Evans, NY

GPS: Bennett Beach: 42.659295, –79.059643

Wendt Beach State Park: 42.677570, –79.050735

FEATURES: Hike among old-growth oaks and hemlocks as they tower on top of 25- to 40-foot-high sand dunes. The more than 300-year-old trees are gnarled and lean inland from the relentless lakeshore winds on Bennett and Wendt beaches. These are "sister" beaches, with Bennett hosting Big Sister Creek while Little Sister Creek flows through Wendt's wooded parkland and into Lake Erie.

DISTANCE: 1 mile, Wendt Beach hike

2.6 miles, Shoreline Trail from Bennett Beach, Wendt Beach, and the Town Park

LEVEL OF DIFFICULTY: Easy

USAGE ICONS—BENNETT BEACH:

BEST SEASONS—BENNETT BEACH:

USAGE ICONS—WENDT BEACH:

BEST SEASONS—WENDT BEACH:

TRAIL MAP: At trailhead kiosk

MANAGED BY: Erie County Parks

Stand at the water's edge and look back at the shore to see the natural dunes with towering trees.

UNIQUE FEATURES

"The Beaches" Shoreline Trail system: A 13-mile bike/hiking trail along the shore of Lake Erie connects these parks and other Lake Erie destinations.

Forty-foot natural sand dunes: Wendt and Bennett Beaches are the only examples in Western New York of Lake Erie's 40-foot-tall natural towering sand dunes, giving you a glimpse of what the shoreline looked like before development.

Sunken wetland forest: An elevated boardwalk takes you through a sunken wetland forest with massive old trees and stumps of great giants.

Eagle sightings: Wendt and Bennett beaches are well-known for eagle sightings. They are often seen soaring near the shoreline.

Ice volcanoes: In January and February, ice volcanoes form near the lakeshore as ice shelves build during long, cold periods. These are rare and starkly frozen expanses of icy cones and cracked ice.

THE HIKE, BIKE, OR DRIVE

There is a method to this summertime travel itinerary. The choice is yours whether to **hike, bike, or drive** this route. Whatever your mode of travel, the **Shoreline Trail** is only a 2.6-mile, one-way trip.

Starting out at Bennett Beach, walk or bike through the boardwalk trail that passes over **Big Sister Creek** and weaves through the woods and **40-foot-tall sand dunes** until you reach the glorious sandy beach. Big Sister Creek is a popular fishing spot, and there is an enforced "no watercraft" rule during the summer. From Memorial Day to Labor Day, lifeguards are on duty, and you'll see many families enjoying an afternoon at the beach.

Big Sister Creek flowing into Lake Erie at Bennett Beach

Hike atop 40-foot ancient dunes along the Lake Erie shore.

After you take a dip in the water, walk to the south (away from the creek), and check out the ruins of the abandoned water treatment plant. Just past this, you'll see the sand dunes, with some reaching as high as 40 feet and—equally impressive—some being **4,000 years old!** These ancient dunes are a habitat for shoreline plants, migratory and nesting birds, and insects. Development has destroyed most of the other dunes along Lake Erie, leaving Bennett and Wendt beaches as the last public land in Western New York to see them.

The beach is not that large of an area to walk; when it's time to head back, walk toward the mouth of Big Sister Creek, and take the creek-side trail back to the footbridge. This is the site of the **1885 Bennett homestead** and The Bluffs and Pine Lodge family summer resorts. All that remains are ruins from the Bennett homestead foundation.

When you're ready to move on, travel along the 2.6-mile Shoreline Trail north toward Wendt Beach Park. Along the way, on nearby Dennis Road, you can find Buffalo Audubon's Ayers-Stevenson preserve, located on Little Sister Creek. This 20-acre preserve is a young wetland forest with an abundance of songbirds that serves as a peaceful stop along the way (GPS: 42.667361, –79.045639).

When you arrive at **Wendt Beach**, you'll immediately notice the Wendt family estate up on the bluff. This boarded-up summer home gives a glimpse into affluent, turn-of-20th-century life. Take a few minutes to explore the grounds around the house. Live like the rich—set up your lawn chairs behind the house and have a grand old picnic!

The trail system at Wendt Beach is **all-access friendly** and is actively used in spring, summer, and fall by the local community. The short .50-mile, paved path passes by towering sand dunes with **ancient oaks growing atop the dunes**. As the boardwalk bridge passes over **Little Sister Creek**, notice how the terrain changes from towering dunes to wetland forest.

The giant trees aren't limited to the dunes. All along the **wetland forest trail** section, you can see massive old trees and stumps of long-gone giants that were more than six feet in diameter!

When you reach the end of the boardwalk trail, head back and walk out through the mouth of **Little Sister Creek** to stroll on the beach for a bit.

As you stand at the water and look back at the shore, you can see the stark comparison of the natural dunes and developed private land. The shore of Wendt Beach is a special place that we must protect and cherish! Nowhere else in Western New York can you see ancient trees atop towering dunes along the shore of Lake Erie.

When you're ready to move on, the Shoreline Trail continues along Lakeshore Road, but there is a side trip that is worth considering. Heading north, you'll pass Sturgeon Point Road. Turn left toward the lake until the road ends at the marina. The little beach area at **Sturgeon Point** is a popular local spot for sunset watching, skipping rocks, and, of course, ice cream. Any trip that ends in ice cream is a good trip!

PLANNING YOUR VISIT

Make this trek an annual **summer** ritual. This is a perfect day out, whether you're beachgoing, biking, hiking, or picnicking. Fall brings uncrowded beaches and trails. Cooler temperatures make this a wonderful **fall** day excursion. Migrating birds can be spotted along the shoreline.

Bundle up in **winter**, as Wendt Beach has great snowshoeing and cross-country skiing trails. This is also a great spot to see the rare ice volcanoes that dot the shoreline of Lake Erie in January and February. Ice volcanoes erupt from underneath coastal ice shelves as wind-driven waves push up through cracks and build tall cones of ice when wintry conditions are just right.

Spring is a favorite time for birders and anglers alike. The most popular species caught along Big Sister Creek are smallmouth bass, catfish, and rainbow trout. For birders, this is a prime viewing and photography spot for spring migratory songbirds, waterfowl, and shorebirds.

Glimpse a rarely seen ice volcano at Wendt Beach.

Wendt Beach Boardwalk trail

HIKING DATES

HIKING NOTES

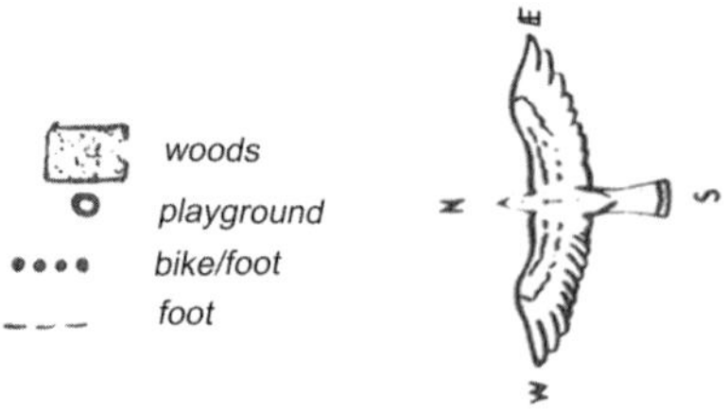

Maps are for overview only; not for directional purposes and not to scale.

12

Weaving Your Way through Walton Woods

LOCATION: Walton Woods, Amherst, NY
GPS: 43.016927, –78.778984

FEATURES: This 7-mile trail system to hike or bike features a 6-acre old-growth forest with more than 150-year-old beech and tulip trees that have massive, 4-foot-diameter trunks. Located near the University of Buffalo, this is an escape into a quiet oasis of nature.

DISTANCE: 1 mile to old-growth forest/loop
LEVEL OF DIFFICULTY: Easy
USAGE ICONS:

BEST SEASONS:

TRAIL MAP: https://bit.ly/SPWNY12
MANAGED BY: Town of Amherst, New York

This might be one of the easiest and most accessible old-growth forests in New York State.

UNIQUE FEATURES

Walton Woods: This 52-acre Amherst park is a peaceful place where you can walk or bike along its miles of paved trails. The park is fairly unknown outside of the close-knit Audubon community whose yards back up to many of the trails.

Walton Woods is home to two lakes, with seven miles of bike and nature trails that wind through the shaded forest. Tucked away and hidden among the young forest and off to the south of Lake Audubon is a rare **six-acre**, **old-growth forest** with more than 150-year-old beech and tulip trees. Several pocket playgrounds are also hidden in the woods, making this a perfect spot to bring kids to unwind.

THE HIKE

Set your GPS for directions to the Amherst Police headquarters, just off the Audubon Parkway. When you arrive, go to the end of the road, and park to the right in Lot F. The paved trail entrance is behind the brown Senior Center sign and is unmarked, which helps to keep it a secret.

The entire trail system could use a map. Luckily for us, the hand-drawn map illustrated here by Bruce Kershner in 1994 will still guide you to the old-growth forest area, as well as show an overview of the trail system and two lakes.

As you enter the paved trail, turn south (right) to first check out the **old-growth forest**. As you head west and away from **Lake Audubon**, you'll come to a fork on the paved path; take the right trail. Two hundred feet later is a "Nature Trail" marker where you'll see the natural footpath through the woods, and, bam, there you are!

As you walk through the old-growth forest, you'll see large, four-foot-diameter beech and tulip trees. Keep strolling straight on the trail, and look through the trees to find the **Princess Leia tree**. It might not be old growth, but this tree definitely has two HUGE growths! Two large burls grow on opposite trunk sides to each other, 20 feet above the ground.

A tiny, tucked-away, 6-acre, old-growth forest at Walton Woods

This short nature trail will cross the paved trail where you can head left to get to the other side of Lake Audubon and return to your car. If you want to continue, turn right and meander along the trails for as long as you like. The trail system seems confusing, but you really can't get lost, as it's all circular. Eventually, you'll end up back where you parked your car.

PLANNING YOUR VISIT

On evening strolls in the **summer**, you can watch fireflies and hear owl hoots and katydid symphonies. It's a bit quieter in the **fall**, except for the crunching of leaves underfoot. The turning autumn leaves are a beautiful sight to see. The paved trails are ideal for snowshoeing, cross-country skiing, or **winter** hiking.

In **spring**, go at dusk and enjoy the chorus of spring peeper frogs for an enjoyable and peaceful evening hike. In **spring** and **early summer**, mallard duck and Canada geese babies are everywhere on the lakes.

HIKING DATES

HIKING NOTES

Bruce Kershner photo bomb

Find the Princess Lela tree.

Artpark State Park lower trail
along the Niagara Gorge

Winter waterfalls at Hobuck Flats

Hobuck Flats at Eighteen-mile Creek truss footbridge

Valentine Flats trail to Pryamid Hill and Skinny Dip Beach

Searching for spring peepers on the Swallow Hollow trail

Zoar Valley's Valentine Flats and Martin's Point

Mt. Seneca trail at Allegany State Park

Descending into Devil's Hole Trail at the Niagara Gorge

Devil's Hole Gulch at
Devil's Hole State Park

Giant mosquito at Griffis Sculpture Park

Driftwood Cave on
Devil's Hole Trail

The Grotto at Eighteen Mile Creek Park

13

Eighteen Mile Creek Gorge: Secret Grottos, Tunnels, Fishing, and Fossils

LOCATION/GPS:
Eighteen Mile Creek Park Trailhead, Hamburg, NY
GPS: 42.706345, –78.893129
Hobuck Flats Truss Bridge, North Evans, NY
GPS: 42.699297, –78.940589
Mouth of Eighteen Mile Creek, North Evans, NY
GPS: 42.711355, –78.966972

FEATURES: The treasures along Eighteen Mile Creek truly are still a secret (shhh!). The gorge has numerous hidden waterfalls; mature stands of sycamore, cherry, oak, and ash; and one of the best fossil-hunting areas on the East Coast of the United States.

DISTANCE: Varies, see each hike
LEVEL OF DIFFICULTY: Varies from easy to challenging, see each hike
USAGE ICONS:

BEST SEASONS:

EIGHTEEN MILE CREEK TRAIL MAP:
https://bit.ly/SPWNY13
MANAGED BY: Erie County Park System, Erie County, New York (Eighteen Mile Creek Park, including the Grotto), New York State Department of Environmental Conservation (Mouth of Eighteen Mile Creek at Lake Erie and Hobuck Flats)

Entering this quiet and magical grotto is like walking into middle-earth.

UNIQUE FEATURES

The grotto: A secluded grotto hides a towering, two-tier waterfall that drops into Eighteen Mile Creek near the confluence of the two creek branches that merge for the final run to Lake Erie.

Cummings Tunnel and Cummings Waterfall: John Cummings was Hamburg's first recorded settler in 1803, setting up his residence on Eighteen Mile Creek after finding the perfect site for a new gristmill at a bend in the creek with a powerful waterfall. Cummings Tunnel, the surviving relic of the mill, can be seen by hiking the creek or from a secret vantage point atop the cliff.

Hobuck Flats truss bridge and Buttermilk Falls: About one mile before the creek reaches the shores of Lake Erie is a historic truss bridge, now a rehabilitated, pedestrian-only bridge that serves as the gateway to this trail system. Buttermilk Falls, a towering, 70-foot waterfall, is to your right on the trail.

Fossils from the gray cliffs of Lake Erie Beach: This is one of the most significant fossil-finding spots in the United States! Whether you want to look for fossils, beach glass, and driftwood, or just float downstream in a kayak, canoe, or tube, this is another secret place where Eighteen Mile Creek flows into Lake Erie, creating a scenic landscape of towering, gray cliff walls and sandy beaches.

THE HIKES

Ideally, you would explore these sites on a few different trips, so you can take in the natural beauty and historical significance each experience offers.

Eighteen Mile Creek Park is the starting point to see the **grotto**, **Cummings Waterfall**, and **Cummings Tunnel**. At the information kiosk, turn left onto the main trail toward the creek. Along the narrow, crumbling asphalt trail, you'll see the gorge uncomfortably close to your right, with meadow to your left.

About 0.25 mile on the trail to your left are old and curious ruins of a long-abandoned homestead with pillars, a foundation, old chimneys, and all kinds of interesting relics. This is a site worth exploring and imagining it in its heyday.

Immediately past the homestead, take the steep path right to the lower trail.

At the bottom, continue walking until you reach the creek bed to see the towering shale cliffs. This is a popular New York State Department of Environmental Conservation (NYS DEC) catch-and-release fishing spot.

Paddlers and anglers enjoy the mouth of Eighteen mile creek.

THE GROTTO

DISTANCE: About 3 miles, round trip

GPS: Parking lot, 42.711355, –78.966972

Hike along the creek to your immediate left, and follow the left creek bank. In summer and fall, you can easily hike in the creek or stay dry hiking the shoreline. There are no trail makers at creek level, so continue to follow the creek about 1.5 miles. You know you're there when you see the north (Evans) branch of the creek merge into the south (Hamburg) branch (the creek you're on).

The short trail to the grotto begins at an opening in the trees just before the two creek branches merge. Going into this little-known, quiet, and magical opening is like walking into middle-earth. Towering above you is a 60-foot, two-tier waterfall, which, depending on the rain levels, can be intense or serene.

If the water levels are low enough, cross the stream to the other shore of the south branch near the confluence to explore further. Here

Hidden at the confluence is the Grotto at Eighteen Mile Creek.

you'll see mature, four-feet-diameter sycamore trees that are typically seen only by a handful of in-the-know anglers and hikers. Now, you're in the know, too.

To get back, just retrace your steps along the south (Hamburg) branch.

SECRET ROUTE TO THE GROTTO

DISTANCE: About .10 mile

GPS: Entrance, 42.700079, –78.90501

Park above the gorge on North Creek Road in Hamburg. You'll see a break in the guardrail on the creek side of the road. Park on the shoulder on the opposite side of the road. Hike down the well-defined trail to reach the creek. Walk to your left to the confluence of the two branches. Cross the creek (only during low-water times), and look for the opening in the trees.

CUMMINGS TUNNEL AND WATERFALL

DISTANCE: About 0.60 mile

GPS: Waterfall, 42.712283, –78.871584

Begin at the same starting point as the grotto hike but turn right, not left. This path is frequented by anglers, so keep dogs leashed and be respectful. As you hike, you'll see towering mature sycamore, oak, and cherry trees at the base of 60-foot cliffs.

At 1.5 miles, you'll come to a sharp bend in the creek and see the low, wide, single-tier Cummings Waterfall. On the right bank, you can see the exit of the 1806 tunnel. If you choose to hike past or through the reasonably traversable waterfall, about an eighth of a mile on your right is the intake to Cummings Tunnel that powered the gristmill's waterwheel. You can also see this "bat cave"-type tunnel entrance from above by driving to the "Hamburg's First Settler" sign on Old Lakeview Road at 42.713506, –78.869774.

Special note: Do not enter the cave, as it's private property with no through-hiking rights.

HOBUCK FLATS TRUSS BRIDGE AND BUTTERMILK FALLS

The trail access is located at Versailles Plank Road in North Evans. Turning onto Versailles Plank Road, go slow as the road turns right and then makes a very sharp left going down a steep hill. At the bottom is a small parking area for the Hobuck Flats Fishing Access Site and the circa 1890s truss bridge that crosses over Eighteen Mile Creek.

BUTTERMILK FALLS

DISTANCE: Easy 0.25 mile from the bridge

GPS: Trailhead, 42.699297, –78.940589

Cross the bridge and follow the well-worn path bearing to your right. Following the creek, you'll soon arrive at Buttermilk Falls, a two-tiered waterfall cascading 69 feet over what are thought to be 370-million-year-old Devonian Shale. The best time to visit is late spring or after a heavy rainfall when the tributary stream is running high and the mosquitoes aren't awake.

Gray Cliffs of Lake Erie

FOSSIL FINDS, GRAY CLIFFS, AND THE HIDDEN LAKE ERIE BEACH

DISTANCE: 0.25 mile through the creek bed

GPS: Parking lot, 42.711355, –78.966972

The gray cliffs of Lake Erie are on Route 5 (Lakeshore Drive) in Evans, New York. Public parking is available at the base of the bridge that crosses Eighteen Mile Creek and is shared by hikers, paddlers, fossil collectors, and anglers.

The best way to see the gray cliffs is to paddle toward the mouth of the lake. You can hike in low water in the summer or fall; however, even in very low water, you'll still need to partially walk in the creek up to knee-high depths. *The hiking option is slippery and mucky and can be difficult.*

Start at the base of the bridge, and head toward the lake. You'll be immediately surrounded by the 60- to 65-foot-high, towering, gray cliffs on the left side of the creek. This area's unique geology has made it a designated Critical Environmental Area by the NYS DEC.

Approaching the lake, the gray cliffs run along both creek banks and up and down the lakeshore. There is an abundance of easily found fossils on the north creek shore, including trilobites, corals, crinoids, brachiopods, and cephalopods from the shallow, trilobite-filled coral reefs of the Devonian-period inland sea.

To the left, you'll see the old pier and staircase ruins used by Frank Lloyd Wright's Graycliff estate. To the right, you get a nice view of the city of Buffalo. *Don't attempt to walk to the other side; the current is swift, and the creek channel is deep.*

Important! Do not dig into the cliffs; this is private property! There are plenty of fossils in the talus (rubble) that have already fallen at the base of the cliffs. Follow the advice of the Fossil Guy for fossil hunting tips: https://bit.ly/SPWNY13Fossil.

PLANNING YOUR VISIT

During **summer** and **fall**, check out Eighteen Mile Creek Park's five-plus-mile trail system and the creek hikes to the grotto and Cummings Tunnel. Hobuck Flats is beautiful in all four seasons. Fossil hunting and paddling at the Gray Cliffs is a perfect summer day activity.

In **winter**, stick to the marked trail systems at Eighteen Mile Creek Park and Hobuck Flats.

Spring is the best time to see Buttermilk Falls at Hobuck Flats.

HIKING DATES

____

____

____

HIKING NOTES

____

____

____

14

Swallow Hollow and the Frog Orgy Experience

LOCATION: 5828 Knowlesville Rd., Oakfield, NY
GPS: 43.125606, –78.325480

FEATURES: A springtime evening walk through the wetlands is abundant with waterfowl, turtles, and frogs. Go at dusk to hear the surreal, haunting choruses of chattering, honking, and hooting from the resident tree frogs, owls, and geese, fondly referred to as an "amphibious orgy."

DISTANCE: 1.3 mile/loop
LEVEL OF DIFFICULTY: Easy
USAGE ICONS:

BEST SEASONS:

TRAIL MAP: At trailhead
MANAGED BY: Iroquois National Wildlife Refuge

Spring peepers pond at Swallow Hollow

Experience a haunting, nighttime spring walk to hear amphibious orgies and cacophonous choruses of spring peepers.

UNIQUE FEATURES

Iroquois National Wildlife Refuge (INWR): Flanked by Oak Orchard Wildlife Management Area and the Tonawanda Wildlife Management Area, this 20,000-acre wetland and waterfowl habitat is the largest in Western New York.

Watch for migratory bald eagles, black tern, black ducks, osprey, and peregrine falcons that use the refuge for nesting, feeding, and resting.

INWR is truly a secret place with several quiet trails to hike, snowshoe, or bird-watch.

Swallow Hollow: This small public-use area and access point to INWR has a 1.3-mile loop trail around and through a wetland and pond with interpretive panels describing the birds, reptiles, insects, mammals, and fauna. An elevated, 0.60-mile boardwalk makes it possible to traverse the wetland and stay dry. It's one of the **longest nature-viewing boardwalks** in Western New York.

The night hike is the "secret" of Swallow Hollow, and those who experience it never forget it. The bizarre sounds of singing, peeping, and chattering frogs (in a state of orgiastic fervor during their "spring break"), combined with honking geese and hooting owls, create a surreal and unique experience.

The night hike is best in late April to early May when the temperature is 48 degrees or higher; otherwise, the frogs will be relatively quiet. Wear headlamps or bring flashlights, but use them as little as possible. Let your eyes get used to the night, and follow the shadows.

THE HIKES

Swallow Hollow Trail: Of course, you *can* hike Swallow Hollow during the day. It's an enjoyable loop, and you're sure to see a nice variety of warblers (up to 22 species spotted!) in the spring and early summer.

To enjoy the night hike, start out about an hour before dusk, and head to your right on the elevated boardwalk. It's an easy walk that little ones and wheeled guests can all enjoy.

The boardwalk will take you through a field as it circles the pond, and a well-worn and marked dirt trail will guide you through a mature, dark spruce forest. You'll veer south and walk through another field, and then walk through a second dark spruce forest.

As the path leaves the forest and turns east, you're the closest to the pond and will hear the chattering, peeping, and nighttime hooting. Walk slowly, and take it all in.

Stop, close your eyes, and "see" the sounds of nature. To head back, cross the footbridge, and walk on the elevated boardwalk back toward your car.

Kanyoo Trail: The trail starts out at the main visitor's center on Casey Road in Basom, New York. Start at the parking lot near the informational kiosk. The trail is actually two loops: a blue-blazed, one-mile-long loop and a yellow-blazed 0.30-mile-long loop.

Start off on the blue loop and head east. This is a well-marked hike with numbered trail posts. The trail has beautiful overlooks for **spotting eagles, terns, and osprey**, as well as a bridge and boardwalk that crosses over Mohawk Pool. Besides the birds of prey, you can often see bluebirds, orioles, and warblers.

Kanyoo Trail at Iroquois National Wildlife Refuge

Looking for eagles? Bald eagles have reclaimed INWR as their home once again! In January, eagles start nesting and continue until eaglets fledge in July. Eagles stay on or near the refuge for most of the year. You're most likely to **observe eagles** in flight from Cayuga and Ringneck Marsh overlooks. Eagle nests are a secret we keep to reduce disturbances to nesting. Check out https://finwr.org/inwr-bird-finder/ for the most recent bird sightings.

PLANNING YOUR VISIT

In **summer**, think bug spray, bug spray, bug spray! If you're up for the adventure, the ponds at INWR make a great breeding ground for fireflies. Swooping in to join the fireflies and other nighttime bugs are hundreds of hungry bats stopping by for dinner. More than eight varieties of bats feed here, including the red bat, silver-haired bat, little brown myotis bat, and the big brown bat.

Look for hundreds of migrating birds stopping over for a rest in the **late fall** (October–November). Snowshoeing is permitted on all trails, and some trails allow for cross-country skiing. This is a quiet, out-of-the-way location in the **winter** where you can find several isolated spots to connect with nature. Hunting and trapping are permitted at INWR, so wear orange in season. **Spring** is peeper time! Remember, the temperatures need to be over 48°F for the frogs to start their singing.

HIKING DATES

HIKING NOTES

Wide, even trails invite wheeled visitors to enjoy.

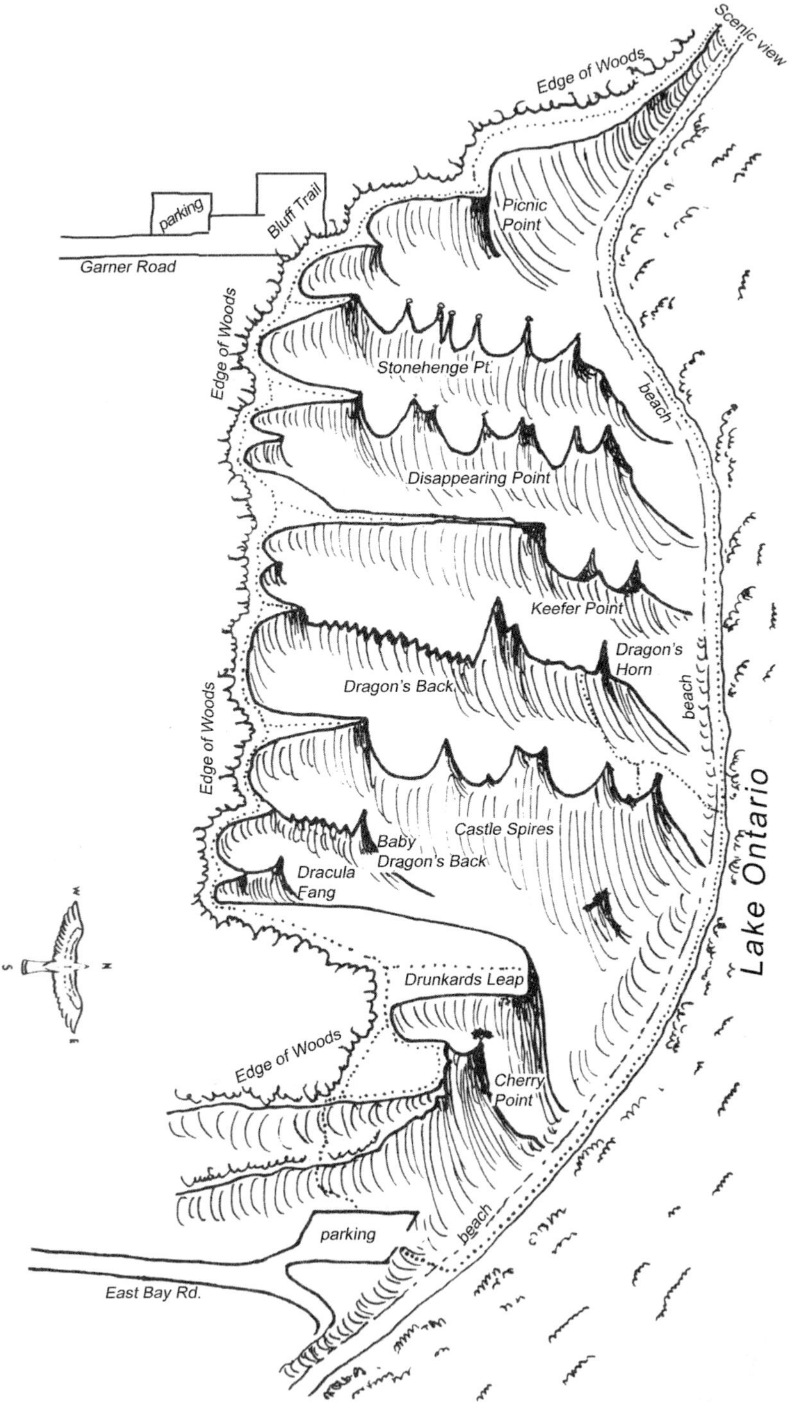

Maps are for overview only; not for directional purposes and not to scale.

15

Bizarre Badlands of New York State: Sodus Point and Chimney Bluffs

LOCATION: Chimney Bluffs State Park, 7700 Garner Rd., Wolcott, NY

GPS: Main entrance: 43.280000, –76.922500,
East Bay Road parking: 43.290382,–76.906408

FEATURES: Sodus Point is called the Badlands of New York, due to the 250-foot-high sand dunes and cliffs with intricately carved-out rock formations from glacial moraine sculpted into spires, dragon backs, knife-edge ridges, and chimneys overlooking Lake Ontario.

DISTANCE: 2.3 miles/loop

LEVEL OF DIFFICULTY: Moderate

USAGE ICONS:

BEST SEASONS:

TRAIL MAP: At trailhead kiosk

MANAGED BY: New York State Parks

Castle Spires and Dragon's Back dune sculptures at Lake Ontario

It looks like a piece of the Dakota Badlands was dropped onto the Lake Ontario shoreline.

A BRIEF HISTORY

Chimney Bluffs were formed by the Ice Age glaciers. The glaciers deposited an elongated hill of compacted gravel known as a drumlin. When the glaciers melted away, Lake Ontario's waters rose and reached the level of the glacial drumlin.

The lake's waters batter the hill during storms, eroding parts of it away, and rains have caused parts of the hill to slide into the lake. The erosion led to the bizarre forms we see today, which continually change due to ongoing erosion and lake water-level changes.

UNIQUE FEATURES

This sculptured fantasy landscape features rock chimneys, spires, dragon backs, knife-edge ridges, vistas, and odd rock formations overlooking the wild shore of Lake Ontario. It's a photographer's delight, and a child and sightseer's paradise, with 250-foot-tall cliffs, intricately and strangely carved by the relentless winds and rains of

Lake Ontario. **This landscape is one of the top natural marvels in the northeastern United States!**

Nine ridges of Chimney Bluffs: They come with fun names such as Drunkard's Leap, Disappearing Point, and Stonehenge Point. Among the odd rock formations are the Dragon's Back, the Dragon's Horn, and Castle of Spires. The knife-edges are as narrow as two inches wide at the top and reach up to 100 feet high.

Shifting sands: Each year, the dune rock formations change from the wind and erosion, making each hike a "new" experience.

THE HIKE

For wheeled visitors, park at the Garner Road entrance, and take the paved path to the water's edge. You'll pass the **sitting tree**, a fun diversion for little ones to climb on. From the end of this short, paved path, you can see the **Chimney Bluffs.** This section of the park is well-groomed and has picnic tables, grills, and bathroom facilities.

The best time to see the nine ridges of Chimney Bluffs is in the late afternoon from the Ridge Trail heading east. To get the **best photos**, you want the dark/light contrast of the shaded ridge lines and gleaming white sand spires.

For those who can hike rough beaches and down 200-plus steps, we recommend parking at the East Bay Road entrance (free, but limited parking) and then scrambling down to the cobble beach. Don't go *UP* the stairs! You'll come down on these stairs on your return. Instead, turn left toward the bluffs, and you'll soon come to the base of these remarkable rock formations. As you pass each one, check out the gullies between the ridges and how each little valley is different. You can often peek inside the bluffs and see the composition of cobble rocks, sand, and limestone that creates these formations.

The beach trail will eventually pass the **badland ridges**. You'll soon get to the section where the ridge is much lower, and the beach is full of massive, bare-trunked trees and large, softball-size cobblestones. Look for the fun **"sandwich" rocks**, layered sandstones with wonderful patterns and colors of red, green, and orange. Lake Ontario stones are the most interesting in Western New York. This is a great spot to sit for a bit and splash around in the water before you climb back up to the main park trail.

East-West and Drumlin Trail is the official ridge trail; if you have time, hike over to **Garner's (Picnic) Point**: it's just a half-mile jaunt, but the hill is quite steep. This fantastic picnic spot gives a **picture-perfect panorama view** from above the badland formations. It's less crowded and a special and secret place.

The entrance to the East-West and Drumlin Trail is well defined and clearly marked. The path will take you past the nine ridge lines. Follow the bluff's edge, but don't get too close to the rim! There are many great photography spots to get the perfect picture. After walking past the nine lines of ridges, the path comes to a downward slope, and 200 cut steps of earth and timbers will take you down and back to your parked car.

PLANNING YOUR VISIT

The **summer** breezes are fantastic, and it's delightful to take a leisurely stroll along the beach trail and splash in the water. In the **fall**, the colors make the bluffs even more amazing! Hunting is permitted in some parts of the park; wear orange and stay on established trails.

Winter is icy and dangerous and not recommended. In May, **spring** forest wildflowers are fantastic, but avoid going after heavy rains.

HIKING DATES

____

____

____

HIKING NOTES

____

____

____

The sitting tree at Chimney Bluffs State Park

Towering trees at
Ganondagan State Park

16

The Town of Peace: Ganondagan, Where the Iroquois Nation Was Born

LOCATION: Boughton Hill Rd., Ganondagan, Victor, NY
GPS: 42.961791, –77.415235

FEATURES: At this sacred site, you can feel the powerful vibrations where the Iroquois Nation was born. Take a reflective walk along the 2-mile "The Earth Is Our Mother" trail, where native plants, used by the Senecas for shelter, fuel, and medicine, can be seen, touched, and smelled.

DISTANCE: 3 miles/loop
LEVEL OF DIFFICULTY: Easy
USAGE ICONS:

BEST SEASONS:

TRAIL MAP: https://bit.ly/SPWNY16. Visit the website for year-round special events. Hiking trails are free; fees may apply for special events and admission to the Seneca Art and Culture Center.
MANAGED BY: New York State Parks and Friends of Ganondagan

Stand atop a 30-acre mesa where, on a clear day, you can see for miles.

UNIQUE FEATURES

The **Iroquois Nations** do not need a book to describe their sacred site, and Ganondagan is not a secret to them, but it is for many of the rest of us! It's the birthplace of a powerful philosophy called the Great Law of Peace, which succeeded in unifying the five tribal nations of the Mohawk, Oneida, Onondaga, Cayuga, and Seneca into the Haudenosaunee Confederacy that survives to this day.

Ganondagan is referred to as the **"Town of Peace"** by the Senecas. Their principles were later adopted by the emerging American democracy, including leaders as servants of the people, citizen participation in government, female suffrage, and nonviolent impeachment of officials.

THE HIKES

The Trail of Peace on Boughton Hill: This figure-eight trail is a short 0.35-mile walk across the Boughton hilltop meadow where once stood the **great longhouse, village, burial places, and livestock**. Reputed as the capital of the Seneca Nation, "Gannagaro" was the prosperous center of Seneca life. This breadbasket and granary community was a center of Iroquois life until it was destroyed in 1687. The story of the

The moon rises over the Great Long House.

Great Law of Peace and the birth of the Haudenosaunee Confederacy is told along the trail, as is the account of the town's destruction by a combined French and Native American army.

The trail is level and lined with interpretive signs and brown trail markers. The meadow area attracts an abundance of birds, bees, and butterflies from the natural plantings of milkweed, wild rose, and native grasses. To continue hiking, next take The Earth Is Our Mother Trail.

The Earth Is Our Mother Trail

The Earth Is Our Mother Trail: Along the two-mile **ethnobotanical trail** are many of the plants used by the Seneca culture. The trail starts directly behind the Seneca Art and Cultural Center, with a paved path that leads to the Long House on Boughton Hill. Follow the trailhead sign into the forest that is filled with hardwood trees, such as hickory, basswood, ironwood, and oak.

There are 29 inscribed plaques next to plants that describe how the Seneca used them, including witch hazel, cattail, spicebush, and wild ginger. The trail goes up and down quiet wooded hills, takes you over a boardwalk, and ends at the Great Brook. If you're seeking a longer hike, then continue on to the red trail marker signs to the Seneca Trail.

Fort Hill and the Granary Trail: This one-mile-round-trip trail can be accessed from the satellite parking lot on Boughton Hill Road (0.80 mile west of the main entrance), or you can hike the **Great Oak Trail** (0.66 mile) and connect to the **Eagle Trail** (0.95 mile) and then intersect with the **Granary Trail** at Fort Hill. If you take the long route, it's just under six miles, round trip. What awaits you, regardless of your journey, is a **30-acre mesa** with a **picketed granary** that the Seneca call *Gah:ha-da-yan-duk* ("a fort was there"). From atop Fort Hill, on a clear day, you can see for miles.

Interpretive signage along the trails

The Seneca built the granary at **Fort Hill** to protect their lives and their mass depository of corn. It's estimated that more than 1,000,000 bushels of corn were stored here and were distributed to towns within the Iroquois Confederacy. In 1687, the French destroyed the granary with all of its corn. Why did they do this? The French were infuriated that the Senecas began fur trading with their British rivals, so they and their indigenous allies aimed to annihilate the Senecas, essentially a genocidal attempt to dominate the international fur trade.

PLANNING YOUR VISIT

Enjoy shaded trails in the **summer,** with tall flowering grasses and shrubs, including yummy raspberry, juneberry, and strawberry plants. The meadow and forests are home to many flying insects, birds, and mammals, including foxes, owls, deer, and butterflies.

As the days and nights become cooler in the **fall**, the trails often get quieter. Walk among mature trees of hickory, beech, walnut, oak, and apple. The migrating birds can sometimes be spotted overnighting in the treetops during the late fall. On a November visit, we were delighted with the surprise sight of *40 to 50 migrating bluebirds resting en masse in the treetops and meadows!* When fall gives way to **winter**, snowshoeing, cross-country skiing, and hiking are encouraged on the trails.

In the **spring**, it may be muddy from spring melt and rain. Wear boots and bring a hiking pole to manage any mucky spots. Hunting is allowed from dawn to 9 a.m. in parts of the park. Always wear orange when hiking during hunting season.

HIKING DATES

HIKING NOTES

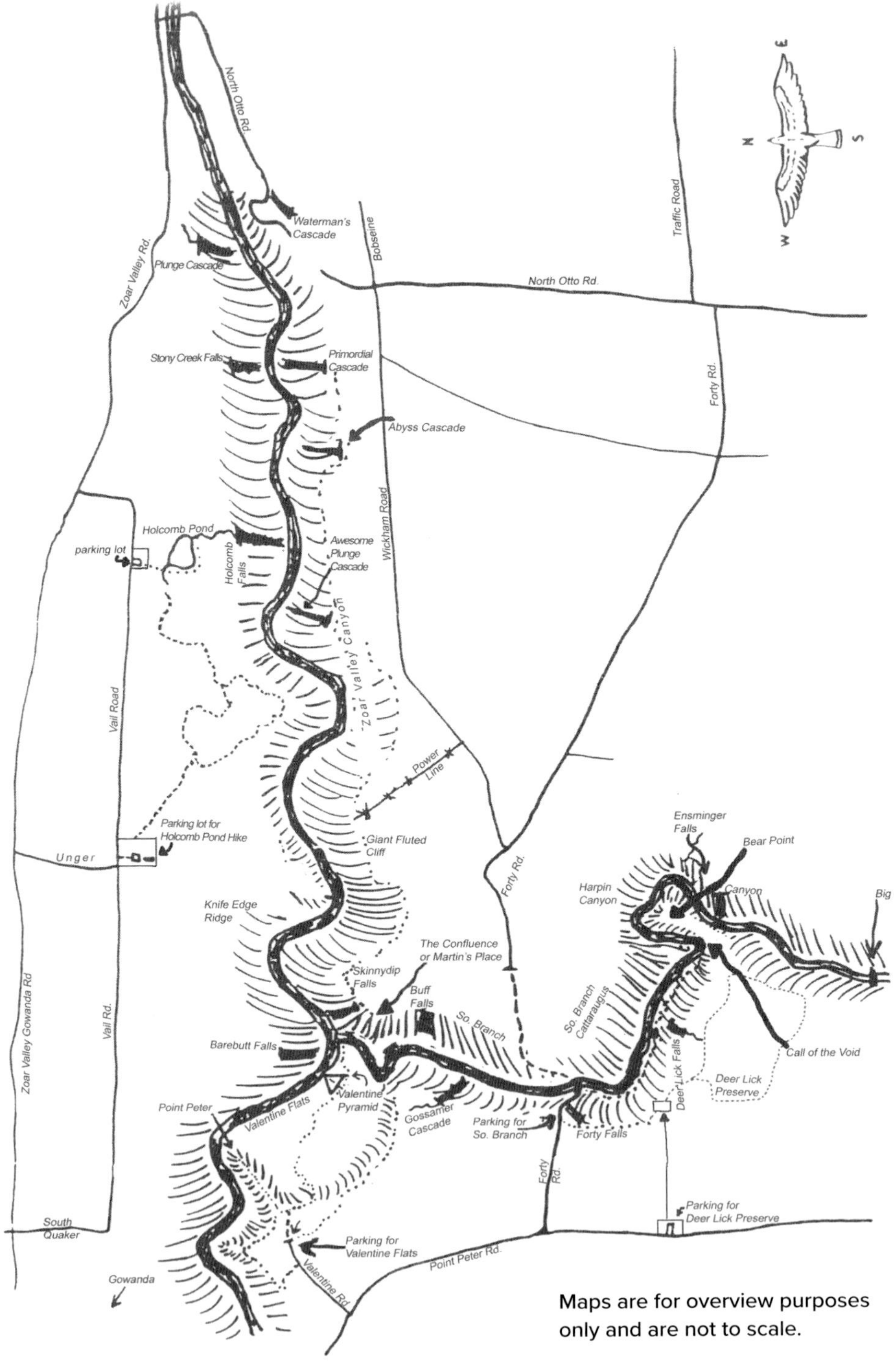

Maps are for overview purposes only and are not to scale.

17

Valentine Flats and Skinny Dip Beach

LOCATION: Valentine Rd., Gowanda, NY
GPS: 42.443657, –78.904134

FEATURES: Still wild and secluded, this beautiful walk guides you along old-growth forest, stunning vistas, sculpted cliffs, waterfalls, and an idyllic swimming hole, dubbed in the 1960s as Skinny Dip Beach.

DISTANCE: 3 miles/out-and-back
LEVEL OF DIFFICULTY: Moderate
USAGE ICONS:

BEST SEASONS:

TRAIL MAP: https://bit.ly/SPWNYZOARVALLEY
MANAGED BY: New York State Department of Environmental Conservation

Skinny Dip Beach at Zoar Valley

The "naturist" areas of Skinny Dip Beach and Barebutt Falls are tamer today than in the 1960s.

UNIQUE FEATURES

Zoar Valley Canyon: The 415-foot-deep canyon is seven miles long and is one of the wildest areas in Western New York! It has more than 400 acres of ancient, mostly virgin, old-growth forest, 20 waterfalls, and a pyramid-shaped hill. The canyons and cliffs were formed by the Main and South branches of the Cattaraugus Creek, which forms the boundary between Erie and Cattaraugus counties.

Valentine Flats: This is a remarkable, terraced, flat area perched *above* the Cattaraugus Creek, but *below*—and completely surrounded by—the towering cliffs of Zoar Valley Canyon. This is a delightful place to experience a "forever wild" piece of nature. No sign of civilization can be seen or heard, except an occasional airplane.

Point Peter: Not for the faint of heart, this wild and wonderful vista is from an extremely narrow rock peninsula 120 feet above Cattaraugus Creek that juts into Zoar Valley Canyon. You'll get the point of why the ridge edge is off-limits.

Skinny Dip Beach: Located at the end of Valentine Flats where the South Branch meets the Main Cattaraugus Creek, this is referred to on official maps as the Confluence. Locals call the south-facing sculpted cliff Martin's Point, The Forks, Indian Head, Indian Face, or Sculpted Ridge. Whatever you call it, it's a spectacular site!

The sculpted, scalloped cliffs rise dramatically from this spot, creating a well-known swimming hole for locals. You're less likely to find skinny dipping today, but for generations, this was the "naturist area to bathe."

Cascades and waterfalls: The waterfalls are best seen and experienced in late spring (March–June) while rafting down the creek. Unless you're an experienced paddler, seek out a commercial, professionally run rafting company.

Skinny Dip Falls: These falls can be seen by hiking 500 feet upstream **on the main branch** from the confluence.

Valentine Pyramid Hill: A unique, 120-foot-high, three-sided pyramid hill. The pyramid shape isn't obvious from the trail, as it's hidden by the thick forest covering. This unique oddity is the only pyramid hill in eastern North America. It was formed when Ice Age glaciers melted and sent massive amounts of water flowing through Zoar Valley. The raging waters carved a channel around the hill, shaping it into the pyramid shape you see today. To understand what lies under the forest covering, check out the 120-foot, sheer cliff walls on the creek side as you stand at Skinny Dip Beach and look west toward the Main creek branch.

THE HIKE

The trailhead and informational kiosk with maps are easy to spot at the trail entrance. Follow the highly visible red trail markers into the ravine, descending 190 feet. Once you come to the field, continue on the trail. You'll pass under **Valentine Arch**, a curved tree that frames the trail—the first of many photo spots.

At the creek's ledge, the trail forks. **Point Peter overlook** is to the left; however, in 2020, the NYS DEC closed sections of the trail, due to erosion. We kept this beautiful and scenic sight in the book, hoping that with remediation and safety precautions, this secret place will once again be open to the public.

As you hike to the right, toward Valentine Flats, be respectful and obey all trail closure and safety signs. *Take the warnings seriously!* Too many hikers and unleashed dogs have fallen to their deaths along the cliff edge.

To reach **Valentine Flats** and **Skinny Dip Beach**, hike along the dirt trail that hugs the upper ledge of the creek. You'll enter a flat meadow with tall grass, wildflowers, and raspberry and blackberry patches. If you go in July and August, the berry picking is a tasty memory!

Soon, you'll pass huge, century-old grapevines that have "grown up" with the trees, giving this trail section the name **"Grapevine Alley."** In front of you, as the path takes a sharp right, away from the creek, you'll be at the base of **Valentine Pyramid**. Climbing is no longer allowed on this hill, due to the extremely dangerous drop-off at the narrow summit. Still, take in the sight of this rare geological formation.

As you round the hill, you enter a section of old-growth forest. On your left, you'll see the giant **Kraken**, a champion, old-growth, oak tree, stretching out its massive trunks in odd formations.

The trail ends at the banks overlooking the **Confluence**. This is where the South Branch intersects with the Main Branch of Cattaraugus Creek. Scurry down onto Skinny Dip Beach and check out the rock formations, splash around in the water, and see the birds that soar above Zoar.

To see either **Skinny Dip Falls** or **Barebutt Falls**, go in early summer during low water flow. Cross the South Branch; once on the opposite side, pass under the cliff and onto the south shore of the Main Branch. Follow it 500 feet upstream (left), and cut into the woods where an inconspicuous stream emerges. Follow the brook 200 feet to Skinny Dip Falls. While there, check out **Valentine Chimney** and **Valentine Cave**.

Barebutt Falls is on the opposite side of Main Branch and 100 feet upstream (left) from the Confluence, where a line of boulders makes the stream shallow. Once across, head straight into the woods for the canyon cliff, 400 feet away. When you reach the cliff bottom, follow it to the left until you reach Barebutt Falls. You'll see the lower of two cascade steps. The upper six steps of the waterfalls aren't visible from the creek.

Return to your car the way you hiked in or continue to hike with the next chapter: *Canyon Country: Cattaraugus Creek and Gossamer Falls.*

PLANNING YOUR VISIT

There's a reason why **summer** is the busiest time of year. The creek is at its lowest, and you can wade in the waters and hike the Main and South branches during low water flow. Weekends often mean hundreds of families and full parking lots. The NYS DEC does close the lot if there are too many cars. **Fall** has absolutely stunning foliage. During the week and mornings, it's quiet, with just a few anglers and hikers enjoying nature.

The site isn't hiked in the **winter** as often, but it's beautiful. *Hunting is permitted; so be sure to wear orange.* If you hike in **spring**, stay away from the swift-flowing creek currents.

Suggested gear includes hiking poles, hiking boots, and splash shoes. If you're going in fall/winter, wear orange; if you're going during snow/ice, wear hiking spikes.

HIKING DATES

____

____

____

HIKING NOTES

____

____

____

Cattaraugus Creek
walk along Zoar Valley

18

Canyon Country: Cattaraugus Creek and Gossamer Falls

LOCATION: Forty Rd. Access Pt., Gowanda, NY
GPS: 42.425369, –78.897204

FEATURES: A beautiful creek hike winds through scenic, 250-foot-deep canyons and passes by three waterfalls. This hike continues to Valentine Flats and Skinny Dip Beach and is a perfect outing for a hot summer day.

DISTANCE: 3.5 miles/loop
LEVEL OF DIFFICULTY: Easy to moderate
USAGE ICONS:

BEST SEASONS:

TRAIL MAP: https://bit.ly/SPWNYZOARVALLEY. Refer to the chapter map for additional details.
MANAGED BY: New York State Department of Environmental Conservation

Hot summer day? This creek hike was meant to cool you off!

Unique Features

South Branch Cattaraugus Canyon: The creek cuts through an impressive 200- to 250-foot-deep canyon until it meets the Main Branch of Cattaraugus Creek at Valentine Flats.

Forty Road Falls: Forty Road Falls plunges 75 feet into the canyon below, and then cascades under the bridge you drive over as you approach the parking area. When you park, the outflow of the falls is on your immediate left with a 10-foot-wide, four-foot-high final cascade into a small pool, just before it enters the creek.

Gossamer Falls: This scenic cascade is a 130-foot-tall white ribbon that drops off the west side of the South Branch of Cattaraugus Creek.

Buff Falls: This 120-foot cascade plunges down the canyon wall. It is opposite the Gossamer Cascade, but not visible from the creek.

THE HIKE

Head toward the creek after checking out the information kiosks. Go down toward the creek and the observation platforms built over the ruins of the old Forty Road Bridge abutment, turn left off the trail, and you'll encounter the outflow of **Forty Road Falls** almost immediately. Because the road actually goes over the falls at the top of the ravine, this is the only close-up view of the cascade. The small pool is just enough for a toddler to splash in or for your dog to get a nice, cold drink.

From here, you can continue two ways: In very low water, you can cross to the other side of the creek for the "far shore hike," following the old logging road into the woods. Heading downstream (to the left), walk 0.25 miles, and look for the view of **Gossamer Falls** on the opposite shore. You'll also be able to find a small trickle flowing from the creek bank. Follow this trickling tributary into the woods 400 feet, and it will take you to the bottom of **Buff Falls.**

Head back out of the woods to the creek's edge, and continue downstream (left) toward **Valentine Flats.** As the canyon walls close in, you're forced to walk in the water or along a thread of dry rocks. After a sharp turn of the creek, the first small swimming hole will appear. Continue to Valentine Flats and join the rest of the swimmers near **Skinny Dip Falls** and **Barebutt Falls** found in Chapter 17, *Valentine Flats and Skinny Dip Beach.*

Alternatively, if you can't or don't want to cross to the far shore, simply turn left at the creek for the "near shore hike" to Valentine Flats, passing **Gossamer Falls** on the way. Depending on water levels, you may be forced into the water, so wear water shoes for this hike!

Go back the same route, or bring two cars to pre-position them at Forty Road and Valentine Flats parking lots.

PLANNING YOUR VISIT

This is a perfect splash hike on a hot **summer's** day (*hike is only possible in low water from June through September*). Wear water shoes with good traction! Go during low water flow only. *Remember: even in low water, the creek has swift currents.* While you won't be able to see the full glory of the various waterfalls, you'll cool off and get to enjoy the stunning gorge views. **Fall** is also a great time to hike the creek. While the water is low, the trees are in full autumn color, and the sun is still warm. **Winter** hiking isn't advised.

HIKING DATES

___

___

___

HIKING NOTES

___

___

___

Fern field at Ross Pond
in Zoar Valley

19

Giant Fluted Cliff and Holcomb Pond

LOCATION: Vail Rd. Access Pt., Gowanda, NY
GPS: 42.451078, –78.879255

FEATURES: A quiet walk through woods, meadows, and ponds that follows the Cattaraugus Creek gorge along the highest point in Zoar Valley. It faces the stunning view of the Giant Fluted Cliff, a 415-foot-tall cliff with dramatic fluted edges.

DISTANCE: 3 miles/loop
LEVEL OF DIFFICULTY: Easy to moderate
USAGE ICONS:

BEST SEASONS:

TRAIL MAP: https://bit.ly/SPWNYZOARVALLEY; refer to the chapter map for additional details
MANAGED BY: New York State Department of Environmental Conservation

Holcomb Pond at Zoar Valley

See the awesome vista of the yawning canyon below you.

UNIQUE FEATURES

Knife Edge Ridge (also known as Hogsback Ridge): This narrow, exposed shale ridge provides an awesome view into the gulf 400 feet below and the Giant Fluted Cliff.

Giant Fluted Cliff: Second-highest cliff in Western New York. At 415 feet high, this unique cliff face is fluted with indentations. Because it faces due north, the sun never shines on it.

Holcomb and Ross Ponds: These boggy ponds are stocked with largemouth bass by the NYS DEC and serve as public fishing access points.

THE HIKE

Before you set out, take note of the sign that this is also the site of the William W. White American Chestnut Plantation. We applaud these efforts to keep this threatened and magnificent species going!

For decades, folks had to bushwhack to enjoy this space. This is no longer needed with the red- and yellow-marked trail system! After you reach the metal gate, follow the grassy trail a short distance to the red trail on your left. If you go in July, enjoy the red raspberries and occasional blackberries along the trail.

The red trail gains elevation at the beginning as it winds through a small pine forest. After less than a half-mile, the trail will branch with a yellow or red option—stay on the red trail to your right. You'll emerge from the woods and cross the berm next to Ross Pond. You'll get a great view of birds feeding, and, depending on the time of year, you'll hear some peepers and croaking frogs.

As you reenter the woods, and the trees become more mature, you'll begin to parallel the edge of the gorge, always staying on the trail, which is safely 15 feet away from the ledge. The view is obstructed in summer, but when the leaves have fallen, you can see the awesome vista of the yawning canyon and a tall, shaded cliff across the way. You're walking above **Knife Edge**. Don't attempt to get any closer or descend the cliff!

Quiet, wooded trail along Zoar Valley

Sun-filled forest wetlands along the trail

From here, in the fall or early spring, you can admire the wilderness and lack of human indicators. You can also see the **Giant Fluted Cliff**, the second-highest cliff in Western New York at 415 feet (Letchworth Canyon is 600 feet).

Dotting the cliffs are massive, old-growth trees, mostly hemlock, that were bypassed as inaccessible during long-gone logging days. Lovingly referred to as the "Gallery of Giants," there are 19 species of trees (surveyed decades ago by coauthor Bruce Kershner), which many old-growth tree experts continue to monitor.

As we got closer to Holcomb Pond on a July hike, we were enchanted with the site of a fern "forest," an expanse of fern and club mosses in a moist undergrowth area. Once you reach the dirt road, **Holcomb Pond** will be in front of you on the other side of the road. The red trail loops around the pond for a beautiful view of feeding birds, turtles, and ducks.

Continue back the way you came, but on the return, take the first yellow trail, which will parallel along Ross Pond for a little bit of a shortcut if you like.

PLANNING YOUR VISIT

In **summer**, the leaves obstruct the view of the gorge and the Giant Fluted Cliff, but the hike is quiet and beautiful. You can forage for raspberries and blackberries in July. **Fall** is always a beautiful time to hike Zoar Valley. Early fall features stunning leaf colors. In late fall, once the leaves are gone, you can see the gorge on the other side and the Giant Fluted Cliff.

In **winter**, the trails are great for a vigorous cross-country or snowshoe hike. The **springtime** view lets you see the opposing cliff and hear the spring peepers. Go before the leaves appear, but when the ground is dry, to avoid the bugs. *Hunting and trapping are permitted here in season, so be sure to wear orange.*

HIKING DATES

____

____

____

HIKING NOTES

____

____

____

Call of the Void at Deer Lick Preserve

20

Deer Lick Preserve and Hair Pin Canyon

LOCATION: Gowanda, NY
GPS: 42.420196, –78.905288

FEATURES: Still wild, this pristine and protected segment of the Zoar Valley Multiple Use Area provides a hike to a view 400 feet above the South Branch of the Cattaraugus River. From this unique cliffside perch, you can see Hair Pin Canyon, watch eagles soar, and listen to Deer Lick Falls cascade 70 feet into the river below.

DISTANCE: 3.2 to 5 miles/loop depending on your route
LEVEL OF DIFFICULTY: Moderate
USAGE ICONS:

BEST SEASONS:

TRAIL MAP: At trailhead
MANAGED BY: The Nature Conservancy

Trees along Bear Point

Take in the deep, beautiful, and wild valley 400 feet below you.

UNIQUE FEATURES

Deer Lick Preserve: This 630-acre, forested nature preserve is located upstream from the other Zoar Valley hikes described in this book. Deer Lick was designated by Congress as a National Natural Landmark because of its ecological significance.

Melissa's Spring Tap: Curb your excitement; the name sounds cooler than the feature, but it's a unique waymarker. At some point, the original pipe became a black hose that drains the high ground of Melissa's Spring to the side of the trail.

Deer Lick Falls: This 70-foot-high falls cascades down the cliff from Deer Lick Preserve to the bottom of Zoar Valley Canyon. You can hear the falls from the white trail, but it's the yellow trail that leads to a view of the top of the falls.

Bear Point: This scenic vista from the ridgeline overlooks Hair Pin Canyon and the South Branch of Cattaraugus Creek.

Call of the Void Amphitheater: The payoff: this view is the reason you came.

Hair Pin Canyon: This 400-foot-deep, sharp-curved canyon is wild and protected from visitors by fierce and feisty landowners. *Fines for treading on this private property are $400!*

The Swinging Seat: Your reward for getting past the halfway point is a fun respite of swinging on this ancient and giant grapevine seat.

THE HIKE

Take the trailhead from the parking lot. All five, well-marked trails start at the same wide, gravel road. As the trail enters the woods, you'll pass a memorial bench on your left. About 0.50 mile in, you'll take the white trail to the right and hike through a mature maple, tulip, and hemlock forest.

A mid-June visit found the distinctive yellow and orange petals of tulip tree flowers littering the trail. Cross Melissa Creek using the

Swinging seat

wooden bridge, and you'll begin ascending the creek valley toward the upper rim. The white trail has an upper and lower loop; during the spring, the upper section is typically drier.

You'll come to **Melissa's Spring Tap**, which is an underwhelming natural seep that drains from a black hose. Depending on the time of year, it can be very mucky, but the spring wetness does produce an abundance of edible, oniony ramps carpeting the hillside. They are so plentiful and pungent, their smell perfumes the air! Continue on the lower white trail toward **Bear Point** or backtrack a bit to switch onto the upper white trail. In the spring, you'll hear, not see, Deer Lick Falls as you approach Bear Point along the upper white trail.

The trail appears to end at the "Posted Nature Sanctuary" sign. But go just a few yards farther uphill where the trail takes a sharp left turn. You've arrived at Bear Point, where the trail begins to circle back.

Hello, Zoar! On your right is **Call of the Void Amphitheater**. This is the reason you woke up today. Take in the deep, beautiful, and wild valley 400 feet below you. Standing here, some hikers have reported a phenomenon known as *l'appel du vide*, which, translated from French, means "The Call of the Void," and is the impulse to hurl yourself to your doom. While unnerving, it's actually a pretty common sensation. Don't hurl; just keep hiking!

It's time to double back and turn at a tree that has a double-arrow white blaze, and or marker. Here you can decide to either take the out-

and-back white trail back or continue on the yellow trail. If you hike the yellow trail, you'll descend and cross the creek, bear left, and hike up the steep creek bank. At the top of the creek bank is where you can view the top of **Deer Lick Falls**.

Crossing through the hemlock forest, the land will level out and your path will pass by the **Swinging Seat**, an ancient grapevine that strung itself between two trees across the path. How many hikers' bums have graced this old grapevine? Imagine the stories it could tell.

Continuing on the hike, you'll pass crazy landscapes of bizarre shapes and forms. The trail will merge back to yellow/white at the conjunction of the loop; follow the white trail straight back to your car.

PLANNING YOUR VISIT

Even in **summer**, this is a seldom-used trail, and you'll find areas of beauty and solitude. Areas near Melissa Creek could be buggy and full of muck. The view from the Call of the Void with **fall** foliage is stunning. Quiet and serene, the **winter** trails require snowshoes or micro spikes with hiking poles. The best time to hear Deer Lick Falls is in the **spring**. The trails can be muddy, but you'll be rewarded with ramps, trillium, trout lilies, and jack-in-the-pulpit.

HIKING DATES

______

______

______

HIKING NOTES

______

______

______

College Lodge pond

21

Towering Ancient Forests along the Continental Divide

LOCATION: College Lodge, 8067 Rte. 380, Brocton, NY
GPS: 42.347919, –79.428225

FEATURES: Hike along a 40-acre grove of old-growth trees, including Eastern hemlock, American beech, black cherry, and sugar maple, that sits on the crest of the Portage Escarpment. This 201-acre preserve on the St. Lawrence River Continental Divide has one side where rain and groundwater drain toward Lake Erie and on to the Atlantic Ocean, and the other side drains toward the Mississippi River and into the Gulf of Mexico.

DISTANCE: 1 mile/loop to see old-growth forests, with more than 4 miles of looped trails
LEVEL OF DIFFICULTY: Easy to moderate
USAGE ICONS:

BEST SEASONS:

TRAIL MAP: https://bit.ly/SPWNY21
MANAGED BY: The Western New York Land Conservancy

Erik Danielson shows an old-growth tree surveyed by Bruce Kershner in 1995 and 2002.

As these giants tower before you, think of the work hundreds of people, going back decades, did to save this land so we can enjoy it today.

UNIQUE FEATURES

Old-growth forest: In 1995 and 2002, Bruce Kershner and Robert T. Leverett surveyed and documented 40 acres of non-logged, old-growth forest on the crest of the Portage Escarpment.

St. Lawrence River Continental Divide: The College Lodge sits on the St. Lawrence River Continental Divide: on one side rains feed creeks that flow to Lake Erie and on to the Atlantic Ocean, while the other side's watershed drains toward the Mississippi River and the Gulf of Mexico.

Rare and endangered plants: This is one of the most stunning spring or summer wildflower walks! Go with a flower guide or phone app to identify various common and rare orchids and carnivorous plants that feed off the forest and decaying bark. The wetlands provide the habitat for bryozoans or freshwater coral and other aquatic life.

THE HIKE

If you park near the College Lodge building, the trailhead sign has a QR code sign-in. Sign in! This is how environmental organizations such as the Western New York Land Conservancy can show donors visitor usage and help secure needed funding. The trails loop and zigzag back on each other. Be sure to take a picture of the trail map before you head out.

The inspirational trail names honor environmental and science rock stars such as Muir, Leopold, and Darwin. Who knows, one day there could be a Kershner trail at this preserve.

Start on Leopold going down a hill, and then pass a wetland area to your right. Soon it will intersect with Muir, and the elevation will take you into the forest. It's along Muir that you'll find the **grove of ancient hemlock**, **beech**, **black cherry**, **and sugar maple trees** that were first documented as old growth in 1995 by Kershner and Leverett for their book, The Sierra Club Guide to the Ancient Forests of the Northeast (2004).

Fern at College Lodge pond

As these giants tower before you, think of the work and unstoppable dedication of hundreds of people, going back decades, to save this land, its old-growth trees, and its rare wildflowers and important natural diversity.

Muir descends into the cross-country skiing trail that will lead you to the swamp/pond area. Here, in the summer, you can find **bladderwort, a carnivorous plant** rarely found in Western New York. Its little yellow flowers can be seen coming out of the water in the pond. With the abundance of flying insects, kids and kids-at-heart have a blast watching the carnivorous plants and imagining the mosquitoes sinking to their doom.

In spring, wildflowers such as trout lilies, trillium, and violets can be found, and in midsummer, the tiny orchids start showing their delicate blooms. It's common to find painters and photographers capturing these dainty and showy flowers.

After reaching the pond, you can take the cross-country skiing trail and loop back to the Lodge parking lot.

PLANNING YOUR VISIT

Every season has something special to offer at College Lodge: The **spring** wildflowers (bring bug spray and muck boots), the stunning orchids in **summer**, and, always, the old-growth trees, standing by as the guardians from the past that will save the future.

HIKING DATES

____

____

____

HIKING NOTES

____

____

____

Ancient hemlocks along Muir trail

Kershner family cobra-riding
at Griffis Sculpture Park

22

Surreal Griffis Sculpture Park

LOCATION: Ashford Hollow, NY
GPS: Mill Valley Rd. entrance: 42.370186, –78.691582
Rohr Hill Road site: 42.385145, –78.682015

FEATURES: Be a kid, or bring a kid, to climb on, in, up, and under hundreds of surreal metal sculptures of naked Amazon women, gigantic insects, and heads, busts, and hands of humans and alien-like creatures. Stroll through hilltop fields and vistas that lead to more than 250 bizarre, beautiful, and bewitching statues, mazes, and sculptures.

DISTANCE: 4 miles/loop (both sites)
LEVEL OF DIFFICULTY: Moderate
USAGE ICONS:

BEST SEASONS:

TRAIL MAP: At trailhead
MANAGED BY: Ashford Hollow Foundation
WEBSITE: https://griffissculpturepark.org for special events, concerts, artists in residence programs, and more.

Taming turtles

This is one of the most unique and weird walks imaginable!

A BRIEF HISTORY

Created by Larry Griffis Jr., the Griffis Sculpture Park was one of the first sculpture parks in the United States. In the 1960s, Griffis went to Rome to learn the art of bronze casting. He became inspired by watching his children play among the ancient ruins of Hadrian's Villa and seeing physical interaction with art in a natural and changing setting. In 1967, after his return to the United States, he founded Griffis Sculpture Park.

Walking the grounds, you can still feel the early 1970s hippie vibe of art mingling with nature from the whimsical sculpture formations. Griffis Sculpture Park is an adventure of the imagination and a great day out to meander the trails, let the kids run free, and get a little dirty, while the dog takes a swim in one of the ponds.

UNIQUE FEATURES

Over **250 steel sculptures** by Larry Griffis Jr. and other international artists reside in the woods, fields, and ponds. The sculptures are arranged by themes. The **Mill Valley Site** has nine themes, and the **rohr hill site** has six themes.

THE HIKES

MILL VALLEY ROAD AND MAIN ENTRANCE

DISTANCE: 2.4 miles/loop

After you pay the modest visitor's donation, continue to the trail entrance on your immediate left. It's easy to spot and has an informational kiosk with a trail map, along with special event information.

You'll start out on the green trail, referred to as the Great Lawn, and you'll loop through a meadow that brings you to the lower pond and field where you'll see several **Nude Bathers** surrounding the pond.

The ponds at Griffis have been used for decades by the Griffis family, friends, and guests for swimming, making this the ideal location for the enormously **Graceful Nude Ladies** of the pond to stretch their limbs and dry in the grass.

As you continue uphill, you'll be drawn to the **Tower**, a 30-foot-tall, 8,000-pound steel rod interactive sculpture. Go inside and look out over the landscape. The best view of the park is looking out from its perch.

This magical park is a kid's dream, where they can climb on everything! The sculptures are cast in steel, aluminum, concrete, rock, and natural formations using trees, all with the intent of interaction.

Stone sculptures at Griffis

Take the green trail to the left as it heads uphill and into the forest. Soon this will become the blue trail, and you'll be walking among **10-foot-tall Amazons.**

If you brought a picnic (which we suggest), the upper hill is about halfway through the hike and is a good time to relax in one of the many quiet areas. It has several distinctive areas: the meadow, the Tower, the Rock Cairn garden, the Griffis Family Heads, the Maze, the Stage, and the Drums.

When you're done exploring, follow the blue trail back down the hill, which will intersect with the dirt road and take you back to the parking lot area where you started out.

ROHR HILL ROAD SITE

DISTANCE: one mile/loop

It might seem that there is no need to walk beyond the **towering, human-like sculptures** that welcome guests, but there is so much more hidden in these woods!

Park in the dirt lot with the rustic bathrooms, then cross the road to the mown trail, and head downhill. You'll pass **seven-foot-high spiders, a massive king crab, and other huge, prehistoric creatures** that are peeking at you from the wooded shadows on your right. As you approach the woods below, follow the trail, and lo-and-behold: take in a **20-foot-long, 10-foot-high aluminum king cobra snake**, ready to strike all who approach! Within this slightly eerie, dark, and shadowy forest are a rhinoceros, giant turtle, and other creatures lurking nearby.

Exit the woods, follow the mowed trail around uphill, and see the **Birds in Flight** and the **towering beings** (human or alien, you choose!), and then conclude your visit by paying respect to the **Royal Family** that overlooks and protects the **Enchanted Mountains**.

PLANNING YOUR VISIT

This is a great midsummer's day hike and picnic to escape modernism or become inspired by the intersection of nature and art. The park has an active **summer** events schedule of arts, music, and family programs. The weekends are a popular time for families to let the kids run free.

There are two glorious weeks in **September/October** that set the Enchanted Mountains of Alleghany on fire with red, orange, and yellow **autumn** foliage. Fall foliage hiking at Griffis should be on every Western New Yorker's and visitor's bucket list!

HIKING DATES

HIKING NOTES

Child's play at the Maze

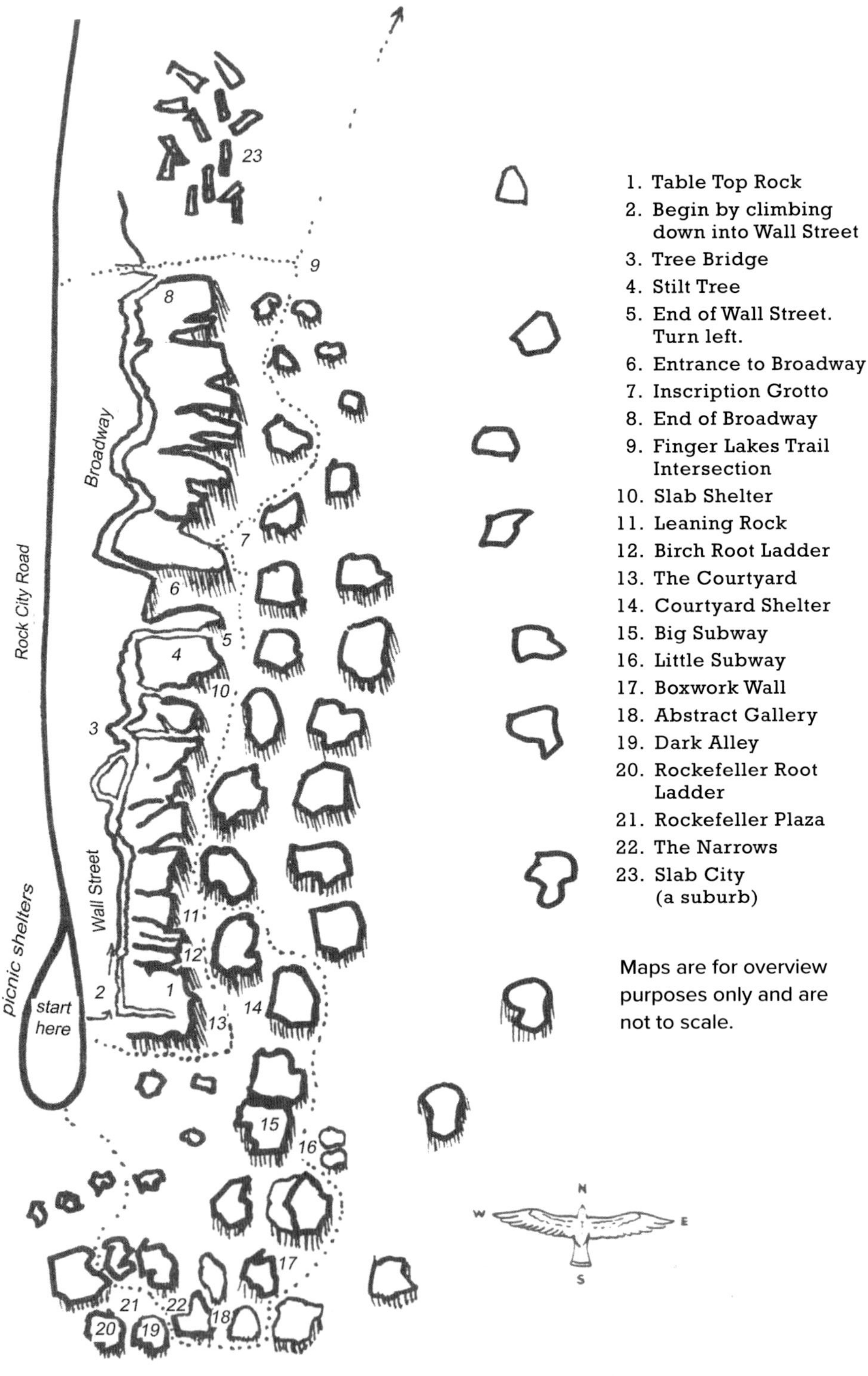

Maps are for overview purposes only and are not to scale.

23

Little Rock City Labyrinth

LOCATION: Little Rock City, Rock City Rd., Salamanca, NY
GPS: 42.208668, –78.708067

FEATURES: Explore a labyrinth of unique and colossal rock formations creating a city-like appearance with boulder-lined alleyways, courtyards, crevices, and caves to explore. Discover and decipher the historic rock carvings from the 1800s. Only a mile long, this hike is a great introduction to the 50-acre park, which is part of the larger, 2,905-acre, Rock City State Forest.

DISTANCE: 1 mile/loop
LEVEL OF DIFFICULTY: Moderate and muddy
USAGE ICONS:

BEST SEASONS:

TRAIL MAP: Refer to the chapter map for additional details.
MANAGED BY: New York State Department of Environmental Conservation

Inscription Grotto, with hundreds of rock carvings

Find the 200-year-old cave carvings while walking through mega-boulder courtyards and tunnels.

A BRIEF HISTORY

Rock cities are unique clusters of megalith rock formations with giant rectangular or sculpted boulders (a.k.a., "buildings") that are arranged in rows, forming fantasy streets, alleyways, and intricate mazes. The rocks are sometimes interlaced with deep crevices and grottos with "secret" rooms. There are 29 rock cities in the region. Little Rock City is the largest and easily accessible at Rock City State Forest (2,905 acres).

UNIQUE FEATURES

Wall Street and Broadway: These are the two longest (two miles long) "streets" of continuous rock-lined corridors.

Little Subway, **Slab Shelter**, **Courtyard Shelter**, **and Leaning Rocks Shelter:** These clusters of boulders feature crevices, caves, and grottos that are fun to crawl into with flashlights.

Inscription Grotto: This grotto has hundreds of historic rock carvings dating to the 1800s. You could spend hours finding and deciphering them.

The Courtyard and Rockefeller Plaza: These two natural courtyards are surrounded by a ring of humongous, building-like boulders.

Birch Root Ladders, Tree Bridge, Stilt Tree, and Picture Frame Roots: These curiosities were created when trees grew through and on rocks stretching high into the sky for light and left their roots pressed against the rock walls to form natural, abstract art.

Slab City and Little Stone City: These "suburbs" are smaller rock croppings located on another ridge, about a half-mile south.

THE HIKE

You must wear boots! Some streets are muddy, even in a dry summer.

When you arrive at the trailhead, continue driving around the loop so your car is facing the way you just entered. The Rock City, with Wall Street, is to your immediate right.

Get oriented, because it's easy to lose all sense of direction in the walled city below. You're at the top of the ridge at an elevation of 2,300 feet. The Rock City lies below the rocks, along the east (left) side of the ridge, and parallels the road.

Important! Don't follow the "Nature Trail" sign; we'll come back that way. If you take this trail first, **Wall Street** and **Broadway** will remain hidden to you. Instead, head into the woods at the immediate left of the **"Little Rock City"** NYS DEC welcome sign.

You'll walk onto a large, flat rock called **Table Top Rock**, which ends at a cliff drop of 20 feet down. Just as you're walking onto Table Top Rock, notice to your left a four- to five-foot-wide crevice between the rocks—this is Wall Street!

Climb down into the crevice, and follow the road and green moss-covered walls as it narrowly winds between, squeezes through, and goes over rock blocks. It's almost always muddy—so muddy you'll sink and squish into it. But don't let that stop you . . . check out every side passageway to find the surprises! Two alleyways lead out of Wall Street and into the forest above, but always come back to Wall Street, or you'll cut your hike short.

Continue through Wall Street, touching the moss-covered walls and admiring the thousands of hanging boulder ferns, giving you the

The entrance to
Wall Street alley

feeling you're in a jungle forest. Soon you'll cross under **Tree Bridge** and then finally **Stilt Tree**, an ancient hemlock pressed into a crevice standing on two tall root trunks.

As Wall Street leads out to the edge of the forest, continue skirting the cliff face on your left, and then make a right-angled turn to the left. A few steps later, you'll be on **Broadway**, a wider street. Enter this corridor and wander your way through until it ends at the forest opening.

At this point, you'll notice the **pink trail blazes** on the trees. The pink blaze is often accompanied by white trail markers as well. Veer to the right, and follow the pink blazes that indicate the Rock City Nature Trail. If you follow the white trail markers to the left, you'll leave Rock City and hike onto the Conservation Trail. This connects Pennsylvania to Niagara Falls and would be a much longer hike than you're prepared for!

The pink trail will weave between rock buildings and along ledges. Further down the trail, you'll reach a large and dramatic overhang that forms an angular grotto about eight feet high and 15 feet deep and is often filled with groundwater. This is **Inscription Grotto!**

Look at the historical carvings. Once you find one, the others will start revealing themselves. There are hundreds of them, dating back almost 200 years. They are even on the sitting rocks under the cliff. The oldest documented ones are "J.D. June 30, 1861," "Moall 1861," and "Maggie Nash, Elmiara, N.Y. Oct. 2, 1886.

The spot you're standing at right now has been a gathering spot for centuries. It makes you wonder whether teens have always snuck off to the woods to hang out. It's fun to imagine the different reasons people gathered and etched their names into the rock. Now that you've seen this, *don't carve any new ones!* When carvings are old, they are historic treasures. When they're new, it's called graffiti.

After you round the corner of Inscription Grotto, you'll see the entrance to Broadway again. A short distance later, make another right-angled turn around another building, and you'll notice the exit to Wall Street.

Just after that, look along the ledge for the **Slab Shelter**, located six feet up and reached by a series of ledge steps. A little further, you'll enter **The Courtyard.** A short distance off the pink trail and onto the white Conservation Trail is **Leaning Rocks Shelter**, the **Birch Root Ladder**, and **Picture Frame Roots.** Right after these, look carefully on your right for the **Courtyard Shelter.** From here, you can see into it through a tiny peephole inside a dark, angular tunnel. Turn right and hug the building, and you'll find the secret entrance to the **Courtyard Shelter.**

Only a few buildings later, look for the **Big Subway** on the right and then the **Little Subway** on the left. These are cave-like tunnels through the boulders that you walk along. Next along the trail are the **Abstract Galleries**, two rock walls with **boxwork.** These are curious erosion patterns that look like contorted ridges, hollows, and pockmarks up to six inches deep, caused by the dissolving of the cement that holds the sand grains together.

Two long and narrow passageways, **Dark Alley** and **The Narrows**, can be found up the trail. Finally, you enter **Rockefeller Plaza**, a whimsical reminder of the famous landmark in Manhattan. Notice its root ladder up the rock face. The pink/white trail will leave this bizarre, Manhattan-themed stone labyrinth and will return you to civilization, or at least to your car.

PLANNING YOUR VISIT

Summer is the best time to visit, because it's the driest. But even in the driest weather, the alleyways and streets remain muddy. The Enchanted Mountains are spectacular in the **fall**, and so is the ride to Little Rock City and the cool-weather hike. Make sure you wear boots and bring a hiking stick and a headlamp.

Important! Hungry Hollow Road and Little Rock City Road are steep dirt roads and are seasonally maintained from May 1 to November 1. *It's not recommended to visit this site from November through May.*

HIKING DATES

HIKING NOTES

Bill and Maya McKeever with corgi Luke, seen through the peep hole view into Courtyard Shelter

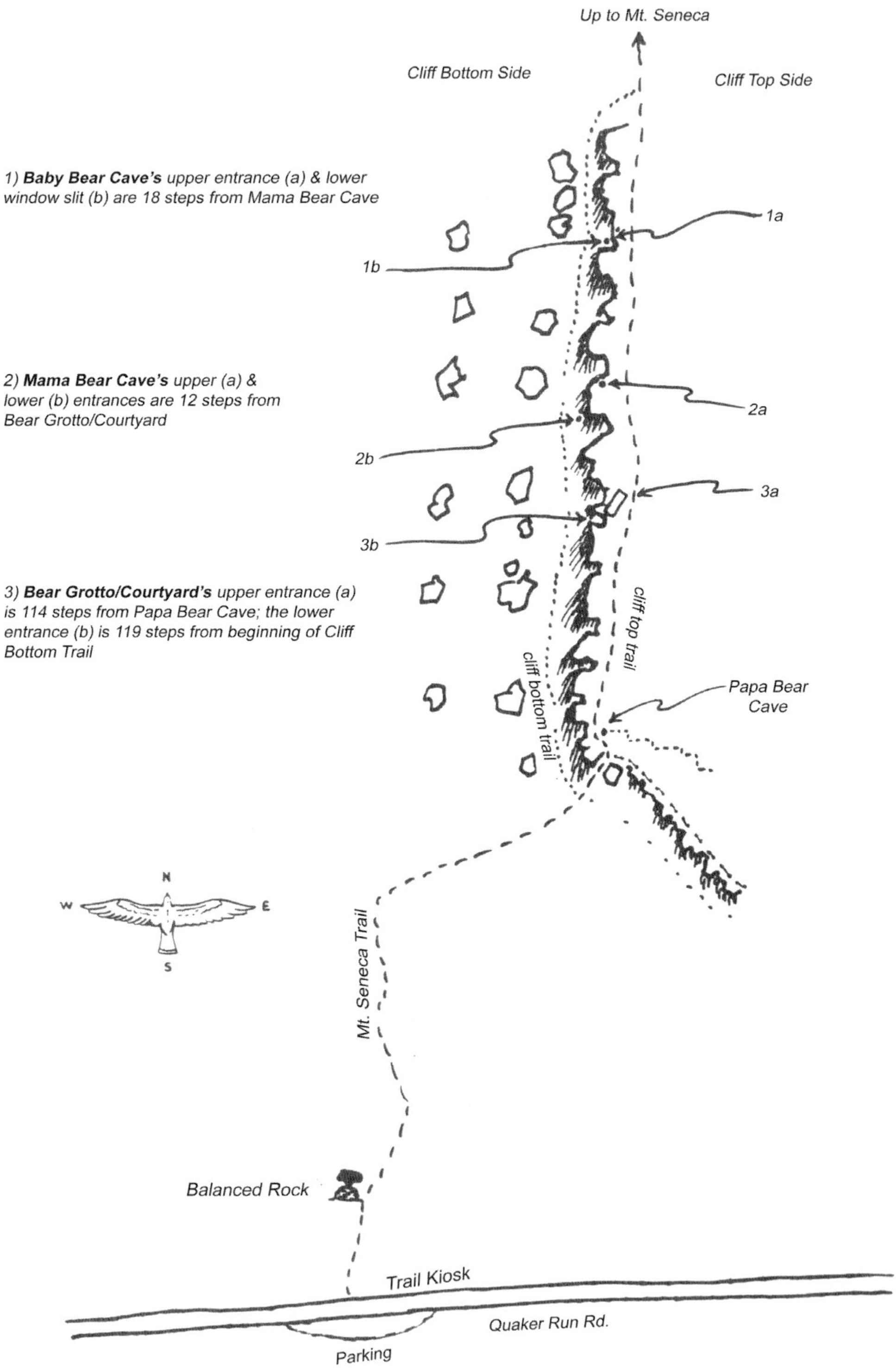

Maps are for overview purposes only and are not to scale.

24

Bear Caves Crawl and Mount Seneca

LOCATION: Allegany State Park, NY
GPS: 42.011080, –78.822982

FEATURES: This mini rock city has four "bear caves" to crawl into and explore. One of the caves is 120 feet long! Be a kid and crawl around to discover natural skylights and a hidden courtyard entrance.

DISTANCE: 4 miles/out-and-back
LEVEL OF DIFFICULTY: Moderate to difficult hike; crawling, twisting, and ducking might be difficult for some.
USAGE ICONS:

BEST SEASONS:

TRAIL MAP: At trailhead; refer to the chapter map for additional details.
MANAGED BY: New York State Parks

Bear Cave Grotto at Allegany State Park

No self-respecting bear uses these caves, just curious humans.

UNIQUE FEATURES

Bear Caves: This is one of 29 rock cities in the region. Bear Caves is smaller than Little Rock City (see this chapter for details), but the caves are deeper!

Papa Bear Cave: This 120-foot-deep cave turns at right angles through tall but narrow "halls." This cave is often wet with water and a little too narrow for "Papa Bear"–sized humans.

Momma Bear Cave: This 30-foot, oblong room is entered from a hole at the top of the cliff. The ceiling is 20 feet high and has a little skylight hole in it. The window at the end provides a peek to the forest outside.

Baby Bear Cave: This is a seven-foot-wide and four-foot-long rectangular room with a unique slit window at its back end. It's fun to call out to others and let them figure out where you are!

Bear Grotto: This 15-foot-deep rock shelter has a short passageway into the back that connects with a small, rectangular, cliff-lined courtyard. The secret courtyard is hidden behind boulders, and you can peer into it from the top.

Mount Seneca: This 2,106-foot peak in Allegany State Park is surrounded by a beautiful wooded forest. While there is no scenic overlook, the forest cover is peaceful and beautiful.

THE HIKE

Take the Red House entrance into Allegany State Park, and park at the trailhead for Bear Caves – Mount Seneca Trail. This is a well-marked trail that climbs in elevation immediately. From the beginning of the trail, the Bear Caves area is 0.25 mile in.

You'll know you've reached the **Bear Caves** when you reach a large collection of giant, square boulders directly in front of you. Before you continue your hike up Mount Seneca, enjoy your time exploring these. But first, you need to find the hidden entrances!

Take the path that climbs up steeply. As soon as you reach the top of the ledge, look for the **Papa Bear Cave** entrance in front of you, on your right just five feet from the trail and 12 feet from the edge of the cliff. The entrance is just two to three feet high and 1.5 feet wide, but it enlarges immediately to the height of an adult. If you can get in, it goes 120 feet deep!

To locate the back entrance of **Bear Grotto**, start walking from Papa Bear Cave's opening along the trail. About 114 adult steps away, you'll notice the box-like Bear Courtyard below you to your left. Climb down into the courtyard to its back end, and you'll find the hidden entrance into **Baby Bear Grotto**.

To reach **Momma Bear Cave**, walk 12 to 15 steps past Bear Courtyard. Step down onto the lower rock shelf, walk to the outer edge of the cliff, and look for a vertical hole in a crevice. This is the entrance! Although it looks unlikely, kids and smaller adults can climb down into it with flashlights. With a bit of twisting and turning, you'll emerge into the cave room.

Once inside Momma Bear Cave, look for the hole in the ceiling and the lower entrance at the back end. While you can exit from here, the

Gnarly tree on Mt. Seneca Trail that resembles an Ent creature from the Tolkien novels

directions to the next cave require you to start from the top entrance of this cave.

Baby Bear Cave is accessed by walking about 18 more steps further from the upper opening of Momma Bear Cave. Look for a vertical opening and drop down into the seven-foot-long and four-foot-wide, rectangular room. At its back end is a narrow window you can peek out into the forest beyond.

Continue your hike up **Mount Seneca** by following the well-marked trail through the woods. In the late spring, there are beautiful wildflowers. For those athletic hikers, this is a great snowshoe hike in the winter.

The Mt. Seneca Trail ends at the road and can be hiked back on ASP-3 to your car.

PLANNING YOUR VISIT

Summer and **fall** are the best time to crawl around the caves without getting too muddy. You can enjoy the nearby streams, too. **Wintertime** is a quiet and heart-pumping snowshoe hike up Mount Seneca. The caves aren't suited for **spring** or **winter** climbing. *Hunting is permitted in-season, so wear orange.* Pack a headlamp and boots for cave exploring.

HIKING DATES

HIKING NOTES

Secret cave entrances from the upper trail

Canadaway Creek
on Lake Erie

25

Canadaway Creek: One of the Last Secret Beaches

LOCATION: Rte. 5 and Temple Rd., Dunkirk, NY
GPS: 42.475277, –79.365650

FEATURES: Canadaway Creek Nature Sanctuary is one of the last wild and undeveloped stretches of Lake Erie. The 33-acre sanctuary protects more than 140 bird species, including the yellow-bellied sapsucker, great blue heron, and more than 22 species of warblers. The creek mouth is on a major bird flyway. In the fall and spring, you can see thousands of birds migrating.

DISTANCE: 0.50 mile/in-and-out
LEVEL OF DIFFICULTY: Easy when dry
USAGE ICONS:

BEST SEASONS:

TRAIL MAP: Not available
MANAGED BY: New York State Department of Environmental Conservation

Catalpa tree on trail

This is the world's most perfect place for skipping rocks.

UNIQUE FEATURES

Spring and fall bird migration: This is a major stopover point for migrating birds in spring and fall and offers protected river stretches for waterfowl.

Shhh . . . secret swimming hole: As the mouth of the creek flows into Lake Erie, the stream turns right sharply and has cut a four- to five-foot-deep, secluded channel that is protected by a sandbar. You can often find local families cooling off in the summer here. You can, too!

Skipping stones: This is a rock-skipping paradise for kids and kids-at-heart. Perfectly round, angled, and flat skipping stones litter the beach in every size. Skip rocks on the creek (but don't anger the anglers!) or, better yet, on the lake.

Shale shelves: If you washed away all the sand and skipping rocks, what lies underneath the lake is a black shale bedrock foundation. Find the saw-toothed layers of stepped bedrock that is reminiscent of a "staircase for giants."

Anglers' delight: Smallmouth bass, steelhead, and brown trout abound here. Steelhead range from the middle of October to May, typically when the sunbathing crowd is long gone.

THE HIKE

Calling this a hike is a bit of an overstatement. Start off by walking down the well-worn dirt path that goes through the woods. Unless you're wearing hip-waders, don't attempt to walk in or along the creek. Trust us, you'll quickly be knee-deep in muck and fishing out your shoes.

There are a few offshoot paths that lead to popular **fishing spots**. Look for the northern catalpa tree, known for its long string bean–like seed pods, and also known as the **worm or bait tree**, along the shore. This tree is often sought out by anglers in June/July for the catalpa moth caterpillar, Ceratomia catalpae (sphinx moth), which is widely regarded as one of the **best live baits**. It's fun to think that local anglers may have planted this for future fishermen.

Within a quarter-mile, you'll reach the beach area. This is one of the best secluded areas to watch the **spring and fall bird migration**. More than 160 bird species have been sighted here, including whistling swan, Caspian tern, wood duck, black-crowned night heron, and 22 species of warblers.

The creek narrows at the beach to only a three- to four-foot gravel spit that almost cuts off the Canadaway Creek. This "sandbar" provides a lovely summer **swimming hole** that locals splash around in. Bring swimsuits if it's going to be a scorcher!

Walking westward (left), you'll find the beach wild and unmanaged. It's littered with driftwood, weathered tree trunks, campfire rings, and little hideaway spots.

The beach is covered with flat and razor-thin rocks in every size. Spending a hot afternoon **skipping stones** and finding the perfect skipper rock on a secluded little beach might be just what everyone needs now and then.

Want to see the bones of Lake Erie? When beaches are unmanaged, the lake currents and winds can strip away the overlying rocks and sand to reveal the bedrock underneath. The black **shale steps** found here are an example of the local bedrock underlying this Great Lake.

PLANNING YOUR VISIT

Summer is best if you want to swim and enjoy the beach. When going in the **spring**, **fall**, and **winter**, be mindful that this is a fishing hotspot. To enjoy the **spring or fall bird migration**, just walk to the beach, find a little hideaway, and sit back and chill for the afternoon. *Spring melt and hard summer rains can make the path mucky and unpassable.*

HIKING DATES

HIKING NOTES

Index by Location and County

Index by Feature